Flutter™ Quick Start

Step-by-step tutorial for crossplatform mobile developers

INTRO

Since 2015, when the Flutter SDK was announced, the popularity of this platform and the Dart language has been steadily growing. The number of articles on this topic is also growing on popular web resources, and many companies are releasing applications created using Flutter™.

The purpose of this book is to teach you how to create cross-platform mobile applications for Android and iOS on Flutter. Using practical examples, we will analyze the basics of the Dart language and the basic principles of building Flutter applications.

This book will be interesting to native mobile developers who are already developing applications, as well as to anyone who wants to start writing cross-platform mobile applications and get to know the Dart language. Only basic programming knowledge is needed. Front-end development experience will come in handy - with it, the course material will be much easier to understand. Nevertheless, it is not necessary to have it at all, especially since after mastering this book you will be one big step closer to being called a front-end development senior.

Scientists from Oxford University have found that only 400 words cover 75% of all English texts. This means that with a vocabulary of 400 of the most used words, in three out of four cases you will know what is meant in any text. This book is written in a similar way: it does not pretend to be a textbook or a complete reference of the Flutter platform and the Dart language. We will not parse each of the widgets in the material library, we will not memorize all the keywords in the Dart language. On the contrary, here are given the most necessary elements, the minimum that a Flutter developer needs to know in production, that is, in an application to solving real problems: creating mobile applications for the real world.

HOW TO WORK WITH THIS BOOK

Empirical information is best absorbed. Therefore, it is expected that you will not just passively read this book, but for each lesson write the code and run the application on two platforms - Android and iOS.

Ideally, try to write your own application, which, for example, will download pictures of cats from the network, or perform a more utilitarian task, let's say, a calculator. At your discretion. In this book we will analyze two examples - first we will create a simple counter, and then more complex - download the weather forecast from openweathermap.org. If you want to write the same application, you will need the KEY API from their site, as well as the Google Maps KEY API. In addition, it is advisable to have experience with Git, Android Studio, Gradle.

There are a total of 10 chapters in the book, the first lessons are simpler, the last are more complex and you may need more time to accomplish them. The already written and working code will help you to understand the course. It is located in the project repository - https://github.com/acinonyxjubatus/flyflutter_fast_start - FlyFlutter Fast Start on the github - there is a separate branch for each lesson. Try not only to copy the code from there, but thoughtfully write it, just checking the code on github. Below is a brief description of the lessons, as well as links to the corresponding branches of the repository.

Lession 1. Launch Flutter [branch *lesson_1_hello_world*]

We will learn how to launch a project on Flutter for Android and iOS, as well as perform simple manipulations with widgets. In addition, we learn how Flutter can be useful and when you can create applications on it.

Lession 2. Dart programming language

We'll go through the basic features and rules of the Dart language.

Lession 3. StatelessWidget and StatefulWidget [branches *lesson-_3_1_stateless_widget, lesson_3_1_stateful_widget*]

We will learn how to create Stateless and Stateful widgets, find out what is a state of widget, and will try to manipulate them. We also learn how to decorate and align widgets.

Lession 4. ListView creation [branch *lesson_4_listivew*]

Let's get acquainted with ListView, find out what are the ways to create it. The knowledge gained would be applied to create a list with weather forecasts.

Lession 5. Loading data from server [branch *lesson_5_http*]

We will learn how to perform asynchronous work in Flutter. We will make a request to the server, receive, parse and show the received information on the client. Thus, we will create a full-fledged client-server application.

Lession 6. Inherited Widgets, Elements, Keys [branch *lesson_6_inherited*]

We will learn what Inherited Widget is, and also will see how it works using an example. We'll figure out what Elements are and how they work. In addition, we will get to know Keys and find out when and how to use them.

Lession 7. Screen navigation, work with Google Maps [branch *lesson_7_navigation_maps*]

We will learn how to switch screens using Navigator. We will be able to connect and show maps from Google Maps in the application, and also connect the additional timezone package necessary in the example.

Lession 8. SQLite, Clean Architecture [branch *lesson-_8_sqlite_clean_architecture*]

We will be able to connect SQLite and save the data in a local database, as well as read them. We will make sure that it is possible and necessary to write clean code in Flutter and write our implementation of the Repository pattern.

Lession 9. BLoC, Streams [branches *lesson_9_bloc, lesson_9_1_counter_bloc*]

We will learn what BLoC is, how it is useful and how to use the bloc library. All this is applicable in practice: we will make a significant refactoring of the weather application, giving the code an appropriate look - we will increase readability and maintainability.

Lession 10. DI, Tests [branches *lesson_10_di_tests, lesson_9_1_counter_bloc*]

We will learn the technique of dependency inversion in relation to Flutter development. In a practical example, we implement the Dependency Injection pattern in Flutter in the weather application example. Then we find out what tests are. We will write unit tests, widget (UI tests) and integration tests for the weather application.

LESSON 1. LAUNCH FLUTTER

In this chapter:

- Cross-platform mobile development
- Why Flutter?
- Setting up environment
- Run Hello World on Android
- Run Hello World on iOS

CROSS-PLATFORM MOBILE DEVELOPMENT

At first let's take a look at Flutter. What is it and why we need it? If you know the answer to the question of what is cross-platform development and Flutter, scroll down to step 3 of this chapter: Setting up the working environment.

It turned out that today in the world of mobile devices 2 platforms iOS from Apple and Google Android are leading. Imagine that right now you need to write a mobile application for both operating systems. You need to hire, conditionally, 1-3 programmers for each platform. Or 5, or 7, depending on the complexity of the project.

Let's take the number 5 for the platform - the optimal, in my opinion, amount for a project of medium complexity. This means 10 programmers in total. Statistically, there will be 2-4 very good, strong programmers, 2-4 weak and 2-4 average, mid-level guys. If the programming language is the same, and the code base is the same, then you can take the best 5 from the same 10 programmers. Of course,

5 programmers will remain out of work, but this is an opportunity to move them to other areas of work, or an additional incentive for them to grow professionally. In other words, by narrowing the scope of work to one codebase, you can simultaneously reduce development costs and increase quality. Of course, this is all theory. In practice, a lot of companies choose native development and are often justified, since only it gives the maximum quality of the final product. But often does not mean always. Let's discuss when and how Flutter can be applied.

WHY FLUTTER?

If you are thinking should you take up the cross-platform and specifically Flutter or not, answer this question: «Why do we need this application, what business goals do we solve with it?» Compare your answer with the two paragraphs below and decide which one your application relates to a greater degree.

To begin with, we will determine in which cases Flutter is not very suitable. In short, these are all cases when the *application is the final product and will compete with other such products* in the application store for top positions. For example, this may be the new Angry Birds, drawing, reader, fitness app. You will need maximum speed, accuracy and smoothness when running the application, and all this gives only the native. It is also worth mentioning the category of applications in which it is planned to actively use the sensors built into the devices, such as Bluetooth, gyroscopes, and a camera. This of course does not mean that Flutter cannot be used in these cases. But it is highly likely that you will have to write native code and / or crutches one way or another.

On the other hand, there are many cases when a real business wants to get a mobile application that will help them implement business processes and/or complement them, but without a fanatical pursuit of a fashionable super-fast UI. An example is loyalty programs, a mobile workplace for employees, an online store, as well as many others, where the *application will serve the real business process*.

In summary, moderate applications with offline business can and should be created on Flutter, and the framework itself is recommended for study by all mobile developers.

SETTING UP ENVIRONMENT

Now, when we've figured out when we can use Flutter, let's learn how to use it!

At first, install Flutter SDK. Download SDK from officail website (https://flutter.dev/docs/get-started/install) Choose your platform (Windows, Mac, Linux) and follow the instruction.

After unpacking add variable into PATH Flutter/bin

```
export PATH"PATH:`pwd`/flutter/bin" // Mac
```

Now you may need to restart your computer.

After installing run in terminal command

```
flutter doctor
```

to make sure you have everything installed correctly.

If you plan to build and test for iOS, then you need to install and up-date Xcode and the corresponding packages using brew. Just following the prompt in the flutter doctor's answer, as well as following macos instruction https://flutter.dev/docs/get-started/install/macos)

If you plan to test on an Android device, then use Android Studio. If you do not have Android Studio, follow nstallation instructions (https://developer.android.com/studio/install) to install it.

RUN HELLO WORLD! ON ANDROID

So, let's start creating the first Flutter application. For this course, you can use Android Studio, Xcode or VS Code - as you wish. We will do it with Android Studio.

Run Android Studio and choose *Start a new Flutter project*

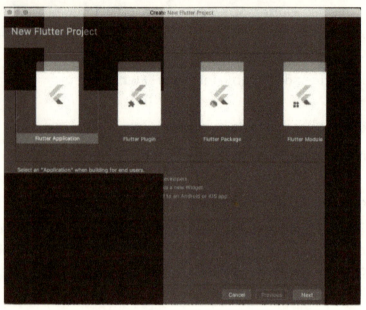

Select **Flutter Application**

Fill down the name *flutter_hello_world* in the **Project Name** field

company domain - **flyflutter.ru** And run Finish

After starting, we immediately see the open file **main.dart**

You may see the line

```
void main()  runApp(MyApp());
```

This is the start point. The **main()** function is the starting point of all Dart applications. Here we are calling the **MyApp** class constructor, which extends from **StatelessWidget**. StatelessWidget is a UI component - widget. We will talk more on Dart language in second lection, and about widgets – in third.

So, on the left we can see the project tree, on the right - the editor. All common Android and iOS code is in the lib folder. Now we have only the main.dart file there

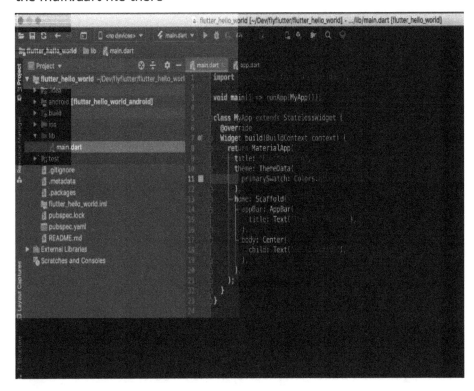

Android Studio has generated a simple increment logic, we will remove it so that it does not confuse us, and replace it with a simpler code

```
import 'package:flutter/material.dart';
void main()  runApp(MyApp());

class MyApp extends StatelessWidget {
  override
  Widget build(BuildContext context) {
    return MaterialApp(
      title: 'Flutter Demo',
      theme: ThemeData(
        primarySwatch: Colors.blue,
      ),
```

```
    home: Scaffold(
      appBar: AppBar(
        title: Text('This is Flutter'),
      ),
      body: Center(
        child: Text('Hello World!'),
      ),
    ),
  );
}
}
```

Now press - Hot Reload – button to apply changes

I must notice that Hot Reload in Flutter is really fast and significantly reduces development time.
Hooray, you should see Hello World on the screen!

Let's analyze the code more deeply. As mentioned above, **MyApp** is inherited from **StatelessWidget**, it is an immutable UI component - a widget. In general, everything in Flutter is widgets, and so is the application. In the widget, we redefine the build method, which indicates what and how to draw.

In our example, we return a MaterialApp object that we created through the constructor. And in the constructor we provide the name, theme and widget home, to which we assign **Scaffold** - the skeleton of the application, which in turn contains appBar and body. An analogy with HTML is appropriate here, where there are also titles and body.

Let's enlarge the text a bit and play with colors:

```
home: Scaffold(
  backgroundColor: Colors.red,
```

```
appBar: AppBar(
  title: Text('This is Flutter'),
),
body: Center(
  child: Text('Hello World!',
    style: TextStyle(
      fontSize: 42.0, //make text bigger
      fontWeight: FontWeight.bold,  // bold
      color: Colors.white, // white
    )
  ),
 ),
),
```

We set the Scaffold widget to a red background, and the text widget applied a style to make it bigger and more visible.

The advantage of Flutter is that the whole logic of working with the application appearance (UI) is written in the code in the same language as the business logic - on Dart. There is no need to get into the resource folder and edit the xml layout.

RUN HELLO WORLD ON IOS

We are writing cross-platform code here! So, let's launch the created application on the iOS device. To do this, simply select the connected iOS device or emulator in the dropdown list and click run

The screen looks amazing, but the unnecessary debug icon gets in the way at the top of the screen, and there's no application icon now. Fix it.

In order to remove the debug ribbon, add the **debugShowChecked-ModeBanner** flag to false in MaterialApp.

```
return MaterialApp(
  debugShowCheckedModeBanner: false,
```

To change the icon, add the package to pubspec.yaml

```
dev_dependencies:
  flutter_launcher_icons: 0.7.4
```

This package will greatly simplify adding icons for two platforms at once. Now we will add the assets folder with an icon in the project root, and also write the path to the icon

```
flutter_icons:
  android: "launcher_icon"
  ios: true
  image_path: "assets/icons/flyflutter_ic_512.webp"
```

don't forget to tell flutter to look at assets folder

```
flutter:

usesmaterialdesign: true
  assets:
    assets/
    assets/icons/
```

Afer that run in terminal commands

```
    flutter pub get
    flutter pub run flutter_launcher_icons:main
```

By this commands we tell the package to create icons

To change the label (icon name) of the application:

For Android - find the manifest in android/app/src/main/AndroidMani-fest.xml and add the line to the application tag

```
android:label"FlyFlutter"
```

For iOS, go to Info.plist under ios> runner / Info.plist and in the key specify the name **CFBundleName**

```
keyCFBundleName/key
stringFlyFlutter/string
```

Done. Run again to verify.

LESSON 2. DART PROGRAMMING LANGUAGE

In this chapter:

- Introduction
- Variables, types and scopes
- Functions
- Constructors
- Inheritance
- Mixins
- Callable classes
- Generics
- synchronous operations
- Exceptions
- Libraries importing
- Compilation

INTRODUCTION

Dart is an open source, high-level, object-oriented general-purpose programming language. It was developed by Google. Influenced by C, Javascript, C #, Java. In it, as in Java and C #, there is a garbage collector. The language supports interfaces, mixins, abstract classes, generics and static typing.

Dart was introduced to the public in 2011 by authors Lars Bark and Kasper Lund. The release of version 1.0 took place in 2013, and version 2.0 was released in 2018

Note: Hereafter in this course, we will review Dart version 2

All Dart applications, like C and Java, have an entry point to main()
functions

```
void main() {
  print('Hello, World!');
}
```

In case you need to run the Dart program from the command line, you
can use the parameterized main:

```
void main(ListString args) {
  print(args);
}
```

VARIABLES, TYPES AND SCOPES

Dart is a type-safe language. It uses both static typing at the compilation time and dynamic verification at runtime of the program. Despite the presence of static typing, it is not necessary to provide the type of a variable. For example, all declarations and initializations below are correct:

```
var name   'Dart';
var year   2011;
String author;
author   "Lars Bark";
ListFoo myList  Foo[];
ListFoo oldList   new List();
```

Note: In Dart 2, the new keyword is optional when declared

SCOPE

By default, all variables have a public scope. There are no keywords that are familiar to Java programmers like *private*, *protected*, and *public* in Dart.

However, if you add the underscore [_] to the variable name, such a variable will have the scope of the library in which it is located.

TYPES

All objects in Dart inherit from the base type **Object**. This is an analogue of Object in Java. It also has a **hasCode()** method and an equivalent of equals, replaced by the comparison operator **==**

The **toString()** method is present in the Object class

Built-in types include:

- Numeric (**num** and his children **int** and **double**)
- Strings
- Booleans
- List
- Set
- Map
- Runes (for expressing Unicode characters in a string)
- Symbols

int - Integer variables. On the Dart virtual machine range is from -2^{63} to $2^{63}-1$

Note: When compiling to JavaScript range becomes from -2^{53} to $2^{53}-1$

double – 64-bit numbers with floating point

int and double are inherits from num

String

Dart string variables are sequences of UTF-16 characters. For initialization, you can use both double and single quotes:

```
var s1  'Single quoted string';
String s2  "Double quoted string";
```

Variable values can be used in rows using the construct

```
{expression}
    var a   2;
    var b   2;
    var s   'a  b  {ab}';
    // output is «224»
```

bool

To create boolean variables in Dart, the **bool** keyword exists. During initialization, you can use the literals true and false. Thus, initialization

```
bool b   0; // incorrect
bool b   true; // correct
```

List

Lists are collections of indexed objects. Examples of declaring and initializing lists:

```
Listint list1   new List();
Listint list2   List();
var list3   [1, 2, 3];
```

For initialization in Dart 2.3, a spread operator is added - an ellipsis - with it you can add many values to the list:

```
var list   [1, 2, 3];
var list2   [0, ...list];
```

Sets

Sets are unordered sets of unique elements. In Dart, in order to create a set, you need to use curly braces for a non-empty set and curly braces in combination with angular and the type of objects for empty:

```
var colors   {'red', 'green', 'blue'}; // initialize it
var colors   String{}; // declaring empty set
SetString colors   {}; // correct too
```

Maps

Maps are key-value data sets. Keys, like values, can be objects of any type. Each key is unique, the values may be different, but may be duplicated. Let's look at an example:

```
var ballGames  {
  'baseball': 'club',
  'basketball': 'hands',
  'football': 'foots'
};
```

Alternative initialization methods

```
var ballGames  Map();
ballGames['baseball']  'club';
...

var ballGames  Map();
ballGames[2]  'hands';
```

Runes

Dart supports runes – unicode symbols. Use if you want to add emoticons. Try this in dartpad

```
Runes input  new Runes('\u{1f60e}');
print(new String.fromCharCodes(input));
```

FINAL AND CONST

Dart also contains keywords **final** and **const**.

If the variable is not planned to be changed, then you should give it the final modifier before the type or word var. Such a variable can be initialized once. Const variables are implicitly considered final. Such variables are used to set constants at the compilation stage.

FUNCTIONS

In Dart, even functions are objects. This means that functions can be assigned to variables and passed as arguments to other functions. The type of the return value is indicated before the function name. This is optional, although recommended:

```
int doubleIt(int value) {
  return value * 2;
}

doubleIt(value) { // correct
  return value * 2;
}
```

Since this function contains only one expression, it can be shortened to one line:

```
int doubleIt(value)  value * 2;
```

Operator => it is a shortening for braces and the **return** keyword.

Optional parameters

When declaring a function, we can specify default values in its signature. For example, we may need to call some function many times with the same parameter, but at the same time we need to maintain flexibility. In this case, when calling from a function with a default parameter, it (this parameter) can be omitted.

There are two types of optional parameters in Dart: *positional* and *named.*

Note: An optional parameter cannot be both positional and named

Named - such parameters can optionally be specified with a name and a subsequent colon and wrapping in curly braces. Example:

```
    updateWidget(int position, { bool withTitle: true, int
padding: 8})
```

@required annotation makes this parameter required

Positional - optional parameters that are placed in square brackets when declaring a function. They will be read when called by their position among the arguments.

```
    String something(String parametr1, [String parametr2])
{
      if (parametr2 ! null) {
        return 'parametr1 and parametr2';
      }     else {
        return 'parametr1';
      }
    }
```

Functions as objects

Functions can be passed as parameters to other functions, and also can be assigned them to variables:

```
    void doubleIt(int it) {
      it   it * 2
      print(it);
```

```
}
var list  [1, 2, 3];
// we pass the function to foreach
list.forEach(doubleIt);

// function as a variable
var doubleIt  (par1)  '{par1 * 2}';
// function as a variable with the type
Function tripleIt  (par1)  '{par1 * 3}';
```

ANONYMOUS FUNCTIONS (LAMBDAS)

Above, we already saw an example of an *anonymous function* - it is a function that does not have a name.

```
var list  ['a', 'b', 'c'];
list.forEach ((it) {
  print('it is {list.indexOf(it)  1} letter of alpha
bet);
 });
```

In this example, we have only one expression in braces, so this entry can be shortened to

```
list.forEach ((it)  print('it is {list.indexOf(it)  1}
letter of alphabet));
```

> Note: Overriding methods (functions) of the parent class is performed using annotation @override

CONSTRUCTORS

Constructors allow you to create an object of the same type as the class in which they are declared. They look like functions:

```
class Rectangle {
  num width, height;

  Rectangle(num width, num height) {
    this.width  width;
    this.height  height;
  }
}
```

Like in Java, if you do not declare a constructor, then the default constructor will be used - without parameters. However, unlike Java, <u>constructors are not inherited</u>.

Constructors may be named:

```
class Rectangle {
  num width, height;
  Rectangle(this.x, this.y)
  Rectangle.square() {
    this.width  10;
    this.height  10;
  }
}
```

When classes inherit from constructors, parent constructors can be called using the construct : super

```
class Rectangle {
  num width, height;
  Rectangle.fromParams(Map params) {
    ...
  }
}

class Square extends Rectangle {
```

```
   Square.fromParams(Map params) : super.fromParams()
{

    ...

   }
```

INHERITANCE

Inhertance is made by keyword extends

There is no *interface* keyword in Dart. Instead, every class implicitly represents an interface (abstract behavior or set of characteristics), which can then be implemented in other classes.

```
   // Musician. The hidden interface contains a method
play()
   class Musician {
    // In the interface
    final instrument;

    // Outside interface - this is a constructor
    Musician(this.name);

    // Inside interface
    void play()  'Hi, I can play instrument';
   }

   // Guitarist implements musician
   class Guitarist implements Musician {
    get name  'Guitar';
    void play()  'Hi, I can play instrument';
   }
```

MIXINS

Mixin in the Dart is a class describing some behavior. It resembles an interface in some ways, but the rules for its use are somewhat different. Mixins are not inherited, but are connected, being "mixed" with the class code, therefore they are called Mixins. The difference from the interface in Java is that mixin methods no longer need to be redefined. Let's look at an example:

```
    // Guitarist implements the musician and knows how to
play different styles
    class Guitarist implements Musician with Jazz, Rock,
Funk {
     get name 'Guitar';
     void play(String arg)   'Hi, I can play arg by
instrument';
    }

    // Mixin
    mixin Rock {
     bool knowsHowToPlayACDC  true;

     void playPopMusic(){
         if(knowsHowToPlayACDC){
         play("TNT")
         }
     }
    }

    mixin Jazz {
     bool knowsHowToEllington  true;

     void playJazzMusic(){
         if(knowsHowToEllington){
         play("Take the A Train)
         }
     }
```

```
}

// mixin Funk
mixin Funk {
  bool knowsHowToPlayBrown  true;

  void playFunkMusic(){
       if(knowsHowToPlayBrown){
       play("I FEEL GOOD!")
       }
  }
}
```

CALLABLE CLASSES

Class objects can be called as functions, if you implement a method call() inside them

```
class ClassAsFunction {
  call(int a, int b)  a*b;
}
main() {
  var classAsFunction  ClassAsFunction();
  var out  classAsFunction(2, 2); // call class as a
function
  print('out'); // will get 4
}
```

GENERICS

Dart has Generic support. They work similarly to Java, and are used in reusable components, for example, in abstractions:

```
abstract class FooT extends BaseClass {
  ...
}
```

Dart has Generics support. They work similarly to Java, and are used in reusable components, for example, in abstractions:

```
var names  ListString();
names.addAll(['Mercury', 'Venus', 'Earth']);
names.add('Mars'); // allowed
names.add(42); // type error
```

ASYNCHRONOUS OPERATIONS

There are **Future** and **Stream** objects in Dart for background work.

Future

Future<T> is an object, which is an asynchronous operation that will return an object of type T after execution. When a function returning Future is called, two steps occur sequentially:

1. This function queues the work that it must do, and immediately returns an outstanding Future object

2. When the operation is completed, the Future object fails with an error or a received value

In order to write an asynchronous function, you need to mark it as **async**, and asynchronous operation itself with the keyword await:

```
import 'dart:async'; // standart asynchronius package

Futurevoid updateData() async {
  var digest  await getDataFromServer(); // we will not
go farther this line until we get a result or error
  print(digest);
}
Note: getDataFromServer() function must return a Fu
ture object too
```

STREAM

If you are familiar with RxJava, then everything should be clear to you from the name. Streams are sequences (Iterable) asynchronous events. Let's look at a simple example:

```
Futureint sumStream(Streamint stream) async { // we get a stream of integers
  var sum  0;
  await for (var value in stream) {
   sum  value;
  }
  return sum;
}

Streamint countStream(int to) async* {
  for (int i  1; i  to; i) {
   yield i; // emit an element
  }
}

main() async {
  var stream  countStream(10);
  var sum  await sumStream(stream);
  print(sum); // result is 55
}
```

The keyword **yield** allow us to emits an element in the *countStream* function, which returns a Stream, that is, it represents a data stream. Then we add each new value from this stream to the sum of the previous ones in the *sumStream* function.

EXCEPTIONS

If you are familiar with Java exceptions, then briefly, all exceptions in Dart are _unckecked_. In other words, all exceptions in Dart occur in Runtime. A function that can throw an exception is not required to declare this in its signature, and it is not necessary to use this function in the _try catch_ block. Another difference from Java is that the type of exception is indicated after the keyword **on**

```
void getException(){
  throw Exception('bam!');
}

try {
  getException();
} on Exception {
  // do something
} catch (e) {
  print('Произошла ошибка: e');
} finally {
  // После слова finally код выполнится обязательно
  closeDatabase();
}
```

When catching exceptions, you can use **on** and **catch**, and both at the same time. catch will be used to access the exception object.

LIBRARIES IMPORTING

To import a library, namespace or class, you must specify the path to them after the keyword import at the top of the file

```
import 'package:shapes/geometric.dart';
import 'package:abstracts/colored.dart' as colored;

...
// Use Rectangle from geometric package.
Rectangle rectangle1  Rectangle();

// use Rectangle from colored package.
colored.Rectangle rectangle2  colored.Rectangle();
```

If you use the above method of loading libraries, they are loaded immediately. To enable them to load on demand (lazy), they can add the **defferd as** modifier

```
import 'package:abstracts/colored.dart' deffered as colored;
```

And then, at the right time, load using the function loadLibrary():

```
Future greet() async {
  await colored.loadLibrary();
  hello.printGreeting();
}
```

COMPILATION

The code written in Dart needs to be compiled for the target platform. Since Dart is a general-purpose language, it can be compiled using either the JIT (Just In Time) pattern or the AOT (Ahead Of Time) pattern.

The difference between JIT and AOT is that with JIT, the code is compiled immediately before use. An example of JIT is JavaScript and the V8 Chromim engine. At the same time, we are not dependent on the architecture of the platform, however, the code will be compiled in runtime, which may take a lot of time and will significantly slow down the performance.

In case of AOT, we compile all the project code in advance and get a binary file. An example is C ++, Java (JVM). At the output, we get a high-speed application, but for one target platform, for another platform, we need another binary.

How does flutter work? Depending on the method of assembly - in different ways. In the case of build release iOS, AOT is used. For release Android, both AOT and CoreJIT (a variation of AOT) can be used.

During development, we want to see changes quickly, and we have such an opportunity - Hot Reload. He just works on the JIT pattern. The platform generates some snapshots, which are then reused.

Pattern / Term	Compilation Pattern	Architecture Specific	Package Size	Dispatch Dynamically
Script	JIT	False	Small	True
Script Snapshot	JIT	False	Smallest	True
Application Snapshot	JIT	True	Lager	True
AOT	AOT	True	Lagest	False

Term / Platform	Android	iOS
Stage	debug	debug
Compilation Pattern	Kernel Snapshot	Kernel Snapshot
Packaging Tool	dart vm (2.0)	dart vm (2.0)
Command	flutter build bundle	flutter build bundle
Packed Product	flutter_assets/*	flutter_assets/*

Term / Platform	Android	iOS	Android(–build-shared-library)
Stage	release	release	release
Compilation Pattern	Core JIT	AOT Assembly	AOT Assembly
Package Tool	gen_snapshot	gen_snapshot	gen_snapshot
Flutter Command	flutter build aot	flutter build aot –ios	flutter build aot –build-shared-library
Packed Product	flutter_assets/*	App.framework	app.so

LANGUAGE SUMMARY

Dart is a powerful development tool that has absorbed a lot of Java, Javascript and other languages that are successfully used in industrial development. Switching to Dart will not be difficult for programmers who wrote earlier in OOP languages, and it is not difficult for beginners to learn it. At the moment, Dart can already be used in release products:

- Flutter – for mobile applications
- AngularDart and Hummingbird for web-development
- Aqueduct for backend

LESSON 3.
STATELESSWIDGET AND
STATEFULWIDGET

In this chapter:

- Everything is widget
- Widget state
- Stateless Widget
- Stateful Widget
- Ephemeral state and App state

EVERYTHING IS WIDGET

Let's start by answering the question "What is Widget in Flutter?". A widget is the main building block of an application user interface. Moreover, these blocks, like nesting dolls, can be nested one into another, forming a nested hierarchical structure. So everything in Flutter is a widget; starting from the text on the button, ending with the application itself, which is also a widget. The main thing that you need to immediately understand about widgets is that by type they are divided into two main categories: **Stateless** and **Stateful**. You can immediately understand what is their difference. Some have a state, others not. Let's dig a little deeper.

WIDGET STATE

State is an "*any information, required for drawing UI at any moment in*

time". As a Java and Kotlin developer, I'm used to writing in an impera-
tive style. For instance,

```
textView.setText("Lorem") or textView.text"Lorem".
```

I changed the appearance of the widget directly, pointing to the system what needs to be changed.

Since Flutter is declarative, the user interface is built as some function
of state:

$$UI = f(state)$$

In other words, the UI is monitoring the State, and if you want to
change the UI, you need to update the state. And here two types of
widgets appear on the scene - those that can change state in runtime,
and those that cannot. It is appropriate here to draw an analogy with
val and *var* variables in Kotlin. Consider StatelessWidget as *val*, and
StatefulWidget as *var* is variable.

STATELESSWIDGET

StatelessWidget cannot change it's state, it is <u>immutable</u>. This type of
widget is convenient to use for static screen elements that need to be
drawn once and not touched anymore. For example, it can be headers,
labels, icons, images from local resources, etc. The most notable example is the application itself. It inherits from the StatelessWidget
class.

However, let's create our StatelessWidget for training. Let it be a simple label with some text.

```
class HintLabel extends StatelessWidget {
  final String text;

  const HintLabel(this.text);

  override
  Widget build(BuildContext context) {
```

```
    return DecoratedBox(
      decoration: BoxDecoration(color: Colors.amber[200]),
      child: Padding(
        padding: const EdgeInsets.all(8.0),
        child: Text(text,
            style: TextStyle(color: Colors.grey[700])),
      ),
    );
  }
}
```

You may notice that the text field is final, and the constructor with the modifier **const**. Thus, we make the text and the instance of the object itself immutable. In the build method, we draw the **DecoratedBox** widget - this is a special widget that inherits from **SingleChildRender-ObjectWidget**, - a widget with one child. It is used to set the appearance of the widget. We do this by pointing to child **BoxDecoration** with the background color. Pay attention to the use of the color gamma of Material. We take amber 300 color. You can learn more about colors on the page. https://material.io/guidelines/style/color.html

Let's now use our new UI component and add it to the main screen.

```
class MyApp extends StatelessWidget {
  override
  Widget build(BuildContext context) {
    return MaterialApp(
      debugShowCheckedModeBanner: false,
      title: 'StatelessWidget sample',
      theme: ThemeData(
        primarySwatch: Colors.amber,
      ),
      home: Scaffold(
        backgroundColor: Colors.amber[300],
        appBar: AppBar(
          title: Text('Labels'),
        ),
        body: Center(
```

```
        child: Column(
            mainAxisSize: MainAxisSize.min,
            mainAxisAlignment: MainAxisAlignment.center,
            crossAxisAlignment: CrossAxisAlignment.
center,
            children: [
              HintLabel('custom label 1'),
              SizedBox(height: 8.0),
              Text('text widget'),
              SizedBox(height: 8.0),
              HintLabel('custom label 2')
            ]),
        ),
      ),
    );
  }
}
```

Launch with Hot Reload and take a glance at our labels

Looks pretty. To check, open the branch *les-son_3_1_stateless_widget*

Let's now create a stateful widget and see how it works.

STATEFULWIDGET

StatefulWidgets appearance can be changed at runtime, because they are mutable. They should be used in the case of text input, slider, checkboxes, etc. To create a new mutable widget, you need to inherit from the StatefulWidget class and create the State class for it. Let's create a simple counter for the experiment.

```
class CounterWidget extends StatefulWidget {
  override
  _CounterWidgetState createState()  _CounterWidget
State();
}
```

In the CounterWidget widget class, we override the **createState** method, returning a state instance in it. And in the state class will be the whole business logic:

```
class _CounterWidgetState extends StateCounterWidget {
  int _count  42; // initial value

  override
  Widget build(BuildContext context) {
    return Container(
        decoration: BoxDecoration(
          borderRadius: BorderRadius.all(Radius.circu
lar(8.0)),
          color: Colors.amber[600],
        ),
        child: Row( // horizontal alignment
          mainAxisSize: MainAxisSize.min,
          mainAxisAlignment: MainAxisAlignment.center,
          crossAxisAlignment: CrossAxisAlignment.center,
          children: [
        IconButton(
              onPressed: () {
                _decrement();
              },
```

```
                  icon: Icon(Icons.remove)),
               Text('_count', style: TextStyle(fontSize:
20.0)),
               IconButton(
                   onPressed: () {
                     _increment();
                   },
                   icon: Icon(Icons.add)),
             ],
           ));
    }

  void _increment() {
    setState(() {
      _count;
    });
  }
  void _decrement() {
    setState(() {
      _count;
    });
  }
}
```

As you remember from the previous lecture, the underscore before the start of a variable indicates that it is private. So in this case, we make the state private for the widget so that only this widget can instantiate it.

The state of the widget is stored in an object of the State class. In which you need to override the **build()** method. When we need to change the state of the widget, we need to call **setState()**, thus saying to it: "re-draw with the new data". We pull this method in the **_increment** and **_decrement** functions, in the lambda, increasing and decreasing the value of the variable, respectively. That's all. Then, in the build method of the widget, at the rendering step, we show the value of the counter in the text box.

```
    Text('_count', style: TextStyle(fontSize: 20.0)),
```

What is interesting here on the UI part?

The buttons for increasing and decreasing the value are represented by the **GestureDetector** widget - in its constructor it receives the **onTap:()** function. In it, in the lambda, we prescribe the call to the **_increment** and **_decrement** functions.

Next, pay attention to how the widgets of the buttons and the counter are located - they are grouped in Row. **Row** is a line where an array of widgets horizontally aligned. Using parameters such as *mainAxisSize, mainAxisAlignment, crossAxisAlignment*, we can set the alignment.

The antagonist of the Row widget is the **Column** widget. As you might guess, it gives us the opportunity to build widgets vertically. If you developed earlier for Android, I'll say right away that we don't have a *RelativeLayout* widget, and *LinearLayout*, instead of them we need to use Row and Column. Well, let's run and check.

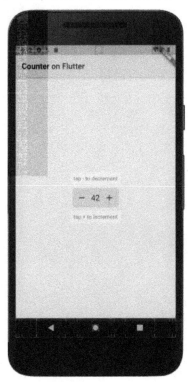

I added our *HintLabels* and also used *Column*, so the App code began to look like this:

```
class MyApp extends StatelessWidget {
  override
  Widget build(BuildContext context) {
    return MaterialApp(
      title: 'Counter',
      theme: ThemeData(
        primarySwatch: Colors.amber,
      ),
      home: Scaffold(
        backgroundColor: Colors.amber[300],
        appBar: AppBar(
          title: Text('Counter on Flutter'),
        ),
        body: Center(
            child: Column(
                mainAxisSize: MainAxisSize.min,
              mainAxisAlignment: MainAxisAlignment.center,
                crossAxisAlignment: CrossAxisAlignment.
center,
                children: [
                HintLabel('tap  to decrement'),
                SizedBox(height: 8.0),
                CounterWidget(),
                SizedBox(height: 8.0),
                HintLabel('tap  to increment')
            ])),
      ),
    );
  }
}
```

EPHEMERAL STATE AND APP STATE

There are two types of states: Ephemeral and Application. It's easier to understand them when viewed as a scope — one for the local level, the other for the global.

Ephemeral state is a state with a widget's scope. Examples: current slidebar progress, currently selected PageView page, checked state at checkbox. In the above example, with the counter, we just used the Empheral state - we stored the count value in the *CounterWidgetState* class and only it knows about the counting.

Application state It is used when it is necessary to transfer data between screens, widgets or user sessions. In this type of state, you can store, for example, business logic data, settings, data downloaded from the server, shopping cart of the online store, etc. For this type of data, there is no strict rule on the storage methodology: you can use setState or Redux, as you wish. The most striking example of using App State is the Inherited Widget. You can store data in it by accessing it from any widget below the hierarchy in the application.

That's all on widgets and their states. In the next lesson, we will create an application with a list of widgets.

LESSON 4. LISTVIEW CREATION

LISTVIEW

In the Quick Start course, we will create an application that will display the weather. In this lesson we will create a weather forecast list for a specific city, and the data will be prepared offline. In the next lesson we will get weather data from the web.

To create a list of items in Flutter, you need to use the **ListView** widget.

There are 4 ways to create it:

1. Using the constructor with the list of widgets ListView (List <Widget> widgets) - use this method only in the case of simple, small static lists, since the ListView will perform calculations for each element of the list, and not only for those visible on the screen.

2. Using ListVIew.builder – suitable for a large (infinite) number of elements, since builder is called only for those elements that are visible on the screen. At input

builder takes the number of elements and callback, with which you need to draw the widget at index i.

3. Listview.separted – for lists with separators between items. Suitable for lists with a fixed number of items.

4. ListVIew.custom – allows you to create a custom list.

To begin, create a simple example by the first method.

CREATING A LISTVIEW USING A CONSTRUCTOR

Since we decided to create a list with a weather forecast, we need at least 2 classes - one for the data model, and one for the weather widget. Create a separate dart file in the same lib folder and add the model class to it to start:

```
class Weather {
  static const String weatherURL  "http://openweatherm
ap.org/img/w/";

  DateTime dateTime;
  num degree;
  int clouds;
  String iconURL;

  String getIconUrl() {
    return weatherURL  iconURL  ".png";
  }

  Weather(this.dateTime, this.degree, this.clouds,
this.iconURL);
}
```

We will load the cloud icon using a convenient and simple method

```
Image.network(weather.getIconUrl())
```

And we form url in the method getIconUrl

In the same file, add the widget class:

```
class WeatherListItem extends StatelessWidget {
  static var _dateFormat  DateFormat('yyyyMMdd - hh:mm');
```

```
 final Weather weather;

 WeatherListItem(this.weather);

 override
  Widget build(BuildContext context) {
    return Padding(
        padding: const EdgeInsets.all(16.0),
        child: Row(children: [
          Expanded(
              flex: 3,
              child: Text(_dateFormat.format(weather.date
Time))),
          Expanded(
            flex: 1,
            child: Text(weather.degree.toString()  " C"),
          ),
          Expanded(
              flex: 1,
              child: Image.network(weather.getIconUrl()))
        ]));
  }
}
```

Expanded widget allows you to align items in a row. The flex parameter sets prioritization, and works much like weight in LinearLayout.

What else is important here? Take a look to _dateFormat.

Using it, we transform the date into a readable string, and it's type is DateFormat, which is prescribed in *intl* package. To use, you need to import it. How it's done?

PACKAGES IMPORT

First you need to add the package name and version to the **pubspec.yaml** file in the dependencies section as follows:

```
dependencies:
  flutter:
    sdk: flutter
```

The following adds the Cupertino Icons font to your application.
Use with the CupertinoIcons class for iOS style icons.

```
  cupertino_icons: 0.1.2

  intl: 0.15.8
```

Next, in the file where you plan to use this package, import

```
    import 'package:intl/intl.dart';
```

All done, the code is compilable.

Now we will use the written widget and model with data. To do this, create a separate application page and set the state for it.

```
class MyApp extends StatelessWidget {
  override
  Widget build(BuildContext context) {
    return WeatherForecastPage("Moscow");
  }
}


class WeatherForecastPage extends StatefulWidget {
  WeatherForecastPage(this.cityName);

  final String cityName;

  override
  StateStatefulWidget createState() {
    return _WeatherForecastPageState();
  }
}

class _WeatherForecastPageState extends StateWeatherFore
castPage {
  ListWeather weatherForecast  [
    Weather(DateTime.now(), 20, 90, "04d"),
```

```
    Weather(DateTime.now().add(Duration(hours: 3)), 23,
50, "03d"),
    Weather(DateTime.now().add(Duration(hours: 6)), 25,
50, "02d"),
    Weather(DateTime.now().add(Duration(hours: 9)), 28,
50, "01d")
];

  override
  Widget build(BuildContext context) {
    return MaterialApp(
      title: 'ListView sample',
      theme: ThemeData(
        primarySwatch: Colors.amber,
      ),
      home: Scaffold(
          appBar: AppBar(
            title: Text('Weather forecast'),
          ),
          body: ListView( // here we pass the list with
elements to the constructor
              children: weatherForecast.map((Weather
weather) {
                return WeatherListItem(weather);
              }).toList())),
    );
  }
}
```

In the **WeatherForecastPageState** state class, we initialized the list with weather objects. The forecast is an array with temperature and cloudiness for every three hours. Then map this list into widgets using the weatherForecast.**map** operator. The created widgets are passed as a parameter to the ListView constructor. Done

CREATING A LISTVIEW USING CONSTRUCTOR A BUILDER

As we remember, the first option to create a list is only suitable for a small number of elements. What if we want to display the weather for a next few weeks? Let's try the second method. Replace the body widget in the build method with the following:

```
body: ListView.builder(
    itemCount: weatherForecast.length,
    itemBuilder: (BuildContext context, int index){
      return WeatherListItem(weatherForecast[index]);
    })),
```

And that's all!

What do we see here? Instead of specifying the entire list at once, in the builder we pass the total number of elements, as well as a callback to draw the i-element at its index. So, ListView will draw only those elements that are visible on the screen.

If we look at the sources of this constructor, we will see there that the callback is a required parameter.

```
      required IndexedWidgetBuilder itemBuilder,
```

The callback itself, or rather its signature, is returned by Widget, and the context and index are accepted as input.

```
/// Signature for a function that creates a widget for a
given index, e.g., in a
/// list.
///
/// Used by [ListView.builder] and other APIs that use
lazilygenerated widgets.
///
/// See also:
///
```

```
///  * [WidgetBuilder], which is similar but only takes a
[BuildContext].
///  * [TransitionBuilder], which is similar but also
takes a child.
typedef IndexedWidgetBuilder  Widget Function(BuildContext
context, int index);
```

The second method should be used in the case of dynamic lists of elements - when you can't say exactly how many elements will be in advance. For example, when data comes from the server.

In case of working with some local resources, when you need to show several elements with icons, it is recommended to use the first approach.

ADDING HEADERS TO LISTVIEW

Let's add the names of the days in front of the weather list items.

To do this, create an abstract class

```
abstract class ListItem {}
```

We will inherit from it the Weather created earlier. Additionally, create a header class. It will be simple and will only contain a date.

```
class DayHeading extends ListItem {
  final DateTime dateTime;

  DayHeading(this.dateTime);
}
```

We also need a widget class for this header:
```
class HeadingListItem extends StatelessWidget implements
ListItemWidget {
```

```
static var _dateFormatWeekDay  DateFormat('EEEE');
final DayHeading dayHeading;

HeadingListItem(this.dayHeading);

override
Widget build(BuildContext context) {
  return ListTile(
    title: Column(children: [
      Text(
        "{_dateFormatWeekDay.format(dayHeading.date
Time)} {dayHeading.dateTime.day}.{dayHeading.dateTime.
month}",
        style: Theme.of(context).textTheme.headline,
      ),
      Divider()
    ]),
  );
}
}
```

Now let's change the initialization code of the list with the weather a little. In the cycle, we will compare the weather items and dates, and, in the case when the day changes, we will add a heading:

```
ListListItem weatherForecast  ListListItem();

override
void initState() {
  var itCurrentDay  DateTime.now();
  weatherForecast.add(DayHeading(itCurrentDay)); // first
heading
  ListListItem weatherData  [
    Weather(itCurrentDay, 20, 90, "04d"),
    Weather(itCurrentDay.add(Duration(hours: 3)), 23, 50,
"03d"),
    Weather(itCurrentDay.add(Duration(hours: 6)), 25, 50,
"02d"),
    Weather(itCurrentDay.add(Duration(hours: 9)), 28, 50,
"01d"),
    Weather(itCurrentDay.add(Duration(hours: 12)), 28, 60,
"04d"),
    Weather(itCurrentDay.add(Duration(hours: 15)), 25, 60,
"03d"),
```

```
    Weather(itCurrentDay.add(Duration(hours: 18)), 28, 60,
"10d"),
    Weather(itCurrentDay.add(Duration(hours: 21)), 22, 60,
"01d"),
    Weather(itCurrentDay.add(Duration(hours: 24)), 28, 60,
"04d"),
    Weather(itCurrentDay.add(Duration(hours: 27)), 21, 60,
"03d"),
    Weather(itCurrentDay.add(Duration(hours: 30)), 28, 60,
"10d"),
    Weather(itCurrentDay.add(Duration(hours: 33)), 28, 60,
"02d"),
    Weather(itCurrentDay.add(Duration(hours: 36)), 27, 60,
"03d"),
    Weather(itCurrentDay.add(Duration(hours: 39)), 28, 60,
"10d"),
    Weather(itCurrentDay.add(Duration(hours: 42)), 24, 60,
"02d"),
    Weather(itCurrentDay.add(Duration(hours: 45)), 20, 60,
"02d")
  ];
  var itNextDay  DateTime.now().add(Duration(days: 1));
  itNextDay  DateTime(
      itNextDay.year, itNextDay.month, itNextDay.day, 0,
0, 0, 0, 1);
  var iterator  weatherData.iterator;
  while (iterator.moveNext()) {
    var weatherDateTime  iterator.current as Weather;
    if (weatherDateTime.dateTime.isAfter(itNextDay)) {
      itCurrentDay  itNextDay;
      itNextDay  itCurrentDay.add(Duration(days: 1));
   itNextDay  DateTime(
          itNextDay.year, itNextDay.month, itNextDay.day,
0, 0, 0, 0, 1);
      weatherForecast.add(DayHeading(itCurrentDay)); //
next heading
    } else {
      weatherForecast.add(iterator.current);
    }
  }
  super.initState();
}
```

Now watch my hands. In the callback of the ListView builder, we adding an *if* - check for the data type, and depending on it we draw either
a header or a weather widget.

```
body: ListView.builder(
itemCount: weatherForecast.length,
itemBuilder: (BuildContext context, int index) {
  final item  weatherForecast[index];
  if (item is Weather) {
    return WeatherListItem(item);
  } else if (item is DayHeading) {
    return HeadingListItem(item);
  } else
    throw Exception("wrong type");
})));
```

In general, this all should be familiar to you if you wrote adapters with
different types of views in Android. Now, move on to the more interesting part: network fetch.

LESSON 5. LOADING DATA FROM SERVER

In this chapter:

- Asynchrony in the Flutter
- Make a server request
- Parse JSON
- Getting a geolocation
- Show the received data

ASYNCHRONY IN THE FLUTTER

Operations such as querying the server, writing data to the database, or determining the geo-location can take a long time. In order not to block the UI with a long synchronous operation, we use asynchronous. In Dart, asynchrony is represented by objects of the **Future** class. A Future object is the result of an asynchronous operation, and can be in two states: *completed* and *uncompleted*. When the asynchronous function is called, we get the Future object in the uncompleted state.

The type of data returned by a Future object is specified in the generic as Future<T>. If you do not need to return a value, you can specify the void type: Future<void>

The function must be marked with the async keyword so that it runs asynchronously. And it will be executed synchronously until it meets the word await

Let's look at an example:

```
FutureResponse performRequest() async {
      var    uri         Uri.https(Constants.BASE_URL,    Con
stants.API_URL);
   return await http.get(uri);
}
```

The function performRequest() executes a request to the server and the result is returned in a future object.

How to use the data received from the server now as they are wrapped in a Future object? Very simple. We need to call the then method on the Future object:

```
void _loadData() {
  _isLoading  true;
  var httpResponseFuture  _performRequest();
  httpResponseFuture.then((response) {
    _isLoading  false; // here the request has already been
completed and we are working with the result
   if (response.statusCode  200) {
      // If everything is OK, parse the json response
}else{
      // error happened
   }
  });
}
```

MAKE A SERVER REQUEST

Above, you have already seen how an asynchronous server request looks like. Let's write it yourself now. For example, we will use the openweathermap API, and at the end of the lesson we will have a real weather forecast application. You must have an API Key to work with thier API, but may use any other cloud API to work with, for instance thecatapi.com

First, register with openweathermap.org to get the API Key.

> Note: Use VPN if domain openweathermap.org is not available in your country.

After registering and receiving the API Key, create a constant file in the project, and add the following lines to it:

```
class Constants {
  static const String WEATHER_BASE_SCHEME  'https://';
  static const String WEATHER_BASE_URL  'api.openweatherm
ap.org';
  static const String WEATHER_IMAGES_PATH  "/img/w/";
  static const String WEATHER_IMAGES_URL
     WEATHER_BASE_SCHEME  WEATHER_BASE_URL
WEATHER_IMAGES_PATH;
  static const String WEATHER_FORECAST_URL  "/data/2.5/
forecast";
  static const String WEATHER_APP_ID  "ваш API ключ";

}
```

We will use the hourly (every 3 hours) forecast for geo-coordinates. Detailed documentation is here. Open the link and copy the example JSON response from the server to the clipboard.

Install the plugin in the studio to convert JSON to Dart

Now we need JSON mapping for classes that represent data from the server. I must say right away that Flutter does not have Gson library, and you need to create classes corresponding to these data and write mapping in them. Writing all this by hands would be tedious and inefficient, so we will use the IDEA plugin, which will do it for us. You can choose any one. Go into the IDE settings, the Plugins section, and in the search type flutter json. I chose FlutterJsonBeanFactory

After installation, restart the IDE.

Create the model package - we will put the classes created on the basis of JSON into it

Right click on the package and select New->JSONtoDartBeanAction

Copy https://openweathermap.org/forecast5#geo5 JSON into plugin popup and click OK. Done, our auto-generated classes are ready to receive information from the server.

Http requests

To perform HTTP requests in Flutter applications you need to use http

<u>package</u>. Update your pubspec.yaml, adding dependency:

```
dependencies:
  http: version number
```

Then run the get packages command, and add the package import to main.dart.

```
import 'package:http/http.dart';
```

A simple GET request would look like this:

```
Futurehttp.Response fetchData() {
  return http.get('API URL');
}
```

In our example, we will use a slightly different construction, since we will need to make a parameterized query. We will take advantage of Uri.https constructor

And our weather request function will look like this:

```
FutureListListItem getWeather(double lat, double lng)
async {
  var queryParameters  { // prepare request parameters
   'APPID': Constants.WEATHER_APP_ID,
    'units': 'metric',
    'lat': lat.toString(),
   'lon': lng.toString(),
  };

  var uri  Uri.https(Constants.WEATHER_BASE_URL,
      Constants.WEATHER_FORECAST_URL, queryParameters);
  var response  await http.get(uri); // execute the re
quest and wait for the result

  if (response.statusCode  200) {
    var forecastResponse
       ForecastResponse.fromMap(json.decode(response.
body));
    if (forecastResponse.cod  "200") {
      // in case of a successful response, parse JSON and
return the list with the forecast
```

```
      return forecastResponse.list;
    } else {
      // in case of an error show an error Scaffold.of(con
text).showSnackBar(SnackBar(
        content: Text("Error {forecastResponse.cod}"),
      ));
    }
  } else {
    // in case of an error show an error    Scaffold.of(con
text).showSnackBar(SnackBar(
      content: Text("Error occured while loading data from
server"),
    ));
  }
  return ListListItem();
}
```

As you remember, we used the coordinates of the current place to get the weather from the API, and passed the latitude and longitude to the getWeather function input. How do we get them?

GETTING GEOLOCATION

To get the current location of the device, connect the package <u>geoloca-tor</u>

```
dependencies:
  geolocator: 5.1.3
```

It allows you to get both the coordinates and the name of the current location of the device. After updating pubspec.yaml add package import

```
import 'package:geolocator/geolocator.dart';
```

Then add the following function to the class with the weather widget:

```
FuturePlacemark getLocation() async {
  Geolocator geolocator  Geolocator()..forceAndroidLoca
tionManager  true;
  Position position  await geolocator
      .getCurrentPosition(desiredAccuracy: LocationAccur
acy.low); // get the geo position
```

```
ListPlacemark placemark  await Geolocator()
    .placemarkFromCoordinates(position.latitude, posi
tion.longitude); // determine the name of the place by
location
  if (placemark.isNotEmpty) {
    return placemark[0]; // we return the first element
from the list of received options
}
  return null;
}
```

It remains only to call the function of determining the coordinates at first, and then get the weather. It will look as follows:

```
void _loadData() {
  _isLoading  true;
  var locationFuture  getLocation(); // get the geoposi
tion future
  locationFuture.then((placemark) { // take value from the
future
    var weatherFuture
    getWeather(placemark.position.latitude, placemark.posi
tion.longitude); // make a request for weather
    weatherFuture.then((weatherData) { // take value re
sponse from theweather future
      initWeatherWithData(weatherData, placemark);
      _isLoading  false;
    });
  });
}
```

That's it, the application can make a request, receive and parse data. It remains to make some changes in the UI so that the widgets created in the last lesson can show the real weather.

SHOW THE RECEIVED DATA

To make the application look more user-friendly, add a progress widget for the duration of downloading data from the server. To do this, add the following functions:

```
Widget get _pageToDisplay {
  if (_isLoading) {
    return _loadingView;
  } else {
    return _contentView;
  }
}

Widget get _loadingView {
  return Center(
    child: CircularProgressIndicator(), // progress widget
  );
}
```

Depending on the state of the load we control by the **_loadData** function, we will either show in the CircularProgressIndicator or the content itself, the list.

Take out a code for creating content from the body of the widget into a separate function:

```
Widget get _contentView {
  return ListView.builder(
      itemCount: _weatherForecast  null ? 0 : _weatherFore
cast.length,
      itemBuilder: (BuildContext context, int index) {
        final item  _weatherForecast[index];
        if (item is ListBean) {
      return WeatherListItem(item);
        } else if (item is DayHeading) {
          return HeadingListItem(item);
        } else
          throw Exception("wrong type");
      });
```

```
}
```

The build method is changed. We removed the ListView creation code from it, and add the call to the **_pageToDisplay** function

```
override
Widget build(BuildContext context) {
  return MaterialApp(
      title: 'Weather report',
      theme: ThemeData(
        primarySwatch: Colors.amber,
      ),
      home: Scaffold(
          appBar: AppBar(
            title: Text(_placeTitle),
          ),
          body: _pageToDisplay));
}
```

We also need to change the rendering code for the widget of the list item so that it takes data not from old mock classes, but from new model - JSON mapping classes.

```
class WeatherListItem extends StatelessWidget implements
ListItemWidget {
  static var _dateFormatTime  DateFormat('HH:mm');

  final ListBean weather;

  WeatherListItem(this.weather);

  override
  Widget build(BuildContext context) {
    return Padding(
        padding: const EdgeInsets.all(8.0),
          child: Row(mainAxisAlignment: MainAxisAlignment.
center, children: [
          Padding(
```

```
          padding: const EdgeInsets.only(right: 16.0),
          child: Text(_dateFormatTime.format(weather.get
DateTime()),
                  style: Theme.of(context).textTheme.sub
head)),
        Image.network(weather.getIconUrl()),
          Text((weather.main.temp.toInt()).toString()   "
\u00B0C",
              style: Theme.of(context).textTheme.subhead)
        ]));
  }
}
```

Done, now you can run.

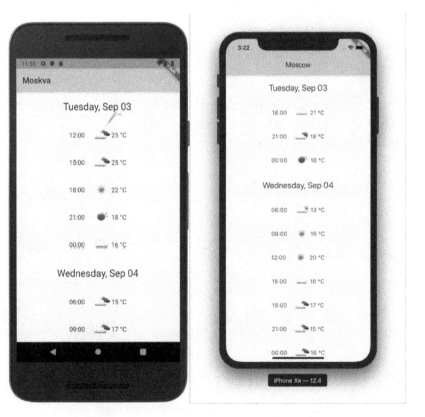

Android   **iOS**

I am not a designer, but it turned out clearly, and shows the current weather. One can use it.

Let's improve usability a bit more and add Pull-To-Refresh. To do this, Flutter has a **RefreshIndicator**

In the content widget, make it root:

```
return RefreshIndicator(
    onRefresh: _onRefresh,
    child: ListView.builder(
```

And into the onRefresh function add this:

```
FutureNull _onRefresh() async {
  CompleterNull completer  CompleterNull();
  var weatherFuture
  _getWeather(_placemark); // make a request for weather
  weatherFuture.then((weatherData) {
    initWeatherWithData(weatherData);
    completer.complete(null);
  });
  return completer.future;
}
```

RefreshIndicator accepts an update function as a parameter, which should return a Future object. This is exactly what we do in the function: We create an object of a special type, **Completer**, which allows us to return the future upon completion of the page refresh. Also, Completer can return an error. The principle of the work of Completer is well described in the documentation:

```
* If you do need to create a Future from scratch — for
example,
* when you're converting a callbackbased API into a Future
based
* one — you can use a Completer as follows:
```

That is, in fact, Completer allows you to create a Future object.

So, we made a request to the server, received, parsed and showed the user the information received on the client. That is, we have created a full-fledged client-server application! At this stage you can already consider yourself as Flutter developers.

LESSON 6. INHERITED WIDGETS, ELEMENTS, KEYS

In this chapter:

- Inherited Widget
- Elements
- Keys

INHERITED WIDGETS

In the third lesson we found out that widgets in a Flutter application form a nested hierarchical structure, starting from the very top level - App. This is convenient when you are making up the screen, but it is extremely inconvenient if we need to transfer data from the top widget to the bottom throughout the hierarchy, or read data from the top widget at the bottom. Here we come to the rescue with a special tool that Google developers have prepared for us - **InheritedWidget**.

If you used below constructions before

```
Theme.of(context).textTheme
MediaQuery.of(context).size
```

then you have already used InheritedWidget. InheritedWidget have a special static of method, which can be called from anywhere down the hierarchy of widgets. This way we can create a central data storage in the application, or AppState.

InheritedWidget class inherits **ProxyWidget** class, which, in turn, inhertits **Widget**.

It describes only one method

```
protected
bool   updateShouldNotify(covariant   InheritedWidget   old
Widget);
```

This is a Boolean method that determines whether to update child widgets.

The provision of data to child widgets is organized using the static method of, which calls BuildContext.inheritFromWidgetOfExactType ([type])

InheritedWidget use pattern:

At first, we 1) create the *MyInheritedWidget* class, inheriting it from InheritedWidget, and add the variable we need to it. InheritedWidget is immutable, that is, its state cannot be changed. How then to update a variable? To do this, create an instance of the MyInheritedWidget class again. And we will create the instance in the 2) specially created StatefulWidget - the MyInheritedWidget wrapper.

We will put all the logic for updating the variable in the State of this widget.

After creating these classes, we need only 3) put the wrapper widget at the root of the application widget hierarchy. And then 4) receive data using the construct

```
var myInheritedWidget  MyInheritedWidget.of(context);
_variable  myInheritedWidget?.myVariable;
```

Any widget in the application hierarchy will have access to it.

If you haven't understood anything yet, it's OK, now we'll look at an example and everything will become clear.

Adding InheritedWidget in the weather app

In the last lesson, we managed to get the geolocation using the geolocator package and then passed the coordinates as parameters to the weather service. However, you may have noticed that the data on the geolocation immediately after receipt was transmitted further along the chain, not being saved anywhere. In fact, we operated on *EmpheralState*. But what if we want to turn to the weather service again without updating the location? After all, the location request usualy takes some time. To solve this issue, we need to save location data at the application level, that is, *AppState*. And here Inherited-Widget will come in handy.

So, perform the above 4 steps:

1) create a class to store the location

```
class LocationInfo extends InheritedWidget {
  final Placemark placemark;

  LocationInfo(this.placemark, Widget child)
      : super(
          child: child,
        );

  // static method to get class instance
  static LocationInfo of(BuildContext context)
      context.inheritFromWidgetOfExactType(LocationInfo);

  override
  bool updateShouldNotify(LocationInfo oldLocationInfo) {
    var oldLocationTime   oldLocationInfo
            ?.placemark?.position?.timestamp?.millisec
ondsSinceEpoch ??
    0;
  var newLocationTime =
    placemark?.position?.timestamp?.millisecondsSinceEpoch ?? 0;


    // compare time in location objects to determine if widgets need to
be updated
  if (oldLocationTime == 0 && newLocationTime == 0) {
    // для случя перой зрузки
    return true;
  }
  return oldLocationTime < newLocationTime;
 }
}
```

2) create a wrapper widget

```
class _LocationInheritedState extends StateLocation
InheritedWidget {
  // local variable
  Placemark _placemark;

  // all location logic is encapsulated in this wrapper
widget
  void _loadData() {
    var locationFuture  getLocation(); // получаем fu
ture на геопозицию
    locationFuture.then((newPosition) {
      // take value from future result
      var placeFuture  getPlacemark(newPosition);
      placeFuture.then((newPlaceMark) {
        onPositionChange(newPlaceMark);
      });
    });
  }

  override
  void initState() {
    super.initState();
    _loadData();
  }

  void onPositionChange(Placemark newPlacemark) {
    setState(() {
      // update local variable
      // and after that the method [build] will be called
      _placemark  newPlacemark;
    });
  }

  override
  Widget build(BuildContext context) {
    // in the build method new [LocationInfo] instance
created
    return LocationInfo(_placemark, widget.child);
  }
```

```
  FuturePosition getLocation() async {
     Geolocator geoLocator  Geolocator()..forceAndroidLo
cationManager  true;
     Position position  await geoLocator.getCurrentPosi
tion(
        desiredAccuracy: LocationAccuracy.low); // get
the geo position
     return position;
  }

  FuturePlacemark getPlacemark(Position position) async
{
     ListPlacemark placemark  await Geolocator().place
markFromCoordinates(
        position.latitude,
        position.longitude); // determine the name of the
place by location
     if (placemark.isNotEmpty) {
       return placemark[
          0]; // return the first element from the list
of received options
     }
     return null;
  }
}
```

3) **Add** LocationInheritedWidget **into the application hierarchy root. Updated main.dart will look like this**

```
import 'package:flutter/material.dart';
import 'package:flutter/widgets.dart';
import 'package:flutter_hello_world/LocationInfo.dart';
import 'package:flutter_hello_world/WeatherForecast
Page.dart';

void main()  runApp(MyApp());

class MyApp extends StatelessWidget {
  override
  Widget build(BuildContext context) {
    return LocationInheritedWidget(
      child: WeatherForecastPage(),
    );
```

```
  }
}
```

4)   Now in **_WeatherForecastPageState** we will redefine the **did-ChangeDependencies** method, which is subscribed to changes in InheritedWidget. Also we will add a location variable.

```
class _WeatherForecastPageState extends State<WeatherForecastPage> {
 // location local variable
 Placemark _placemark;

 bool _isLoading = false;

 Completer<void> _refreshCompleter;

 @override
 void initState() {
  super.initState();
  _refreshCompleter = Completer<void>();
  _loadData();
 }

 Future<void> _onRefresh() async {
  var weatherFuture =
    getWeather(_placemark.position.latitude, _placemark.position.longi-
tude);
  weatherFuture.then((_weatherForecast) {
   initWeatherWithData(_weatherForecast, _placemark);
  });
  return _refreshCompleter.future;
 }

 // the method is called when the state of the objects on
which this widget depends changes
  override
  void didChangeDependencies() {
    super.didChangeDependencies();

   // get the InheritedWidget instance
    var locationInfo  LocationInfo.of(context);
    // read the location from there
    _placemark  locationInfo?.placemark;
```

```
    // load weather forecast
    _loadData();
  }

 void _loadData() {
    // show progressBar while location is null
    _isLoading  true;
    if (_placemark  null) {
      return;
    }
    var weatherFuture  getWeather(_placemark?.position?.
latitude,
        _placemark?.position?.longitude); // make a weather
request
    weatherFuture.then((weatherData) {
      // take value response from weather future
      initWeatherWithData(weatherData, _placemark);
      _isLoading  false;
    });
  }     // the rest stays the same
        * * *
```

Start...

From the user's point of view, everything remains the same, but we now have **InheritedWidget** under the hood.

ELEMENTS

So what's hidden under the hood?

InheritedWidget contains a list of links to all widgets that depend on it. Whenever InheritedWidget is recreated and its data changes, it notifies all widgets from the list. How does this happen? Take a look at the InheritedWidget class. In it we see a line

```
override
InheritedElement createElement()  InheritedElement(this);
```

The **Element** class instance created for a InhertedWidget.

We'll make a small digression here and first look at what Element is.

The class description begins like this:

```
/// An instantiation of a [Widget] at a particular loca
tion in the tree.
///
/// Widgets describe how to configure a subtree but the
same widget can be used
/// to configure multiple subtrees simultaneously because
widgets are immutable.
/// An [Element] represents the use of a widget to config
ure a specific location
/// in the tree. Over time, the widget associated with a
given element can
/// change, for example, if the parent widget rebuilds and
creates a new widget
/// for this location.
```

That is, the UI elements that you see on the screen are nothing more than the objects of the Element class, which are described by the Widget class. It is Elemtents that form the tree of objects on the screen.

Element Lifecycle:

1) Element is created by Widget.createElement

2) The framework calls the ***mount*** method, adding an element to the tree in the appropriate place. From this moment, the elem-

ent becomes **active** and can appear on the screen.

3)   Next, the *update* method can be called on the element in the case when the bound widget changes its state. In case when runtimeType changes (another type of widget) or the key of the element, then you must first call *unmount* on it and then re-inflate.

4)   To deactivate an element, its parent can call *deactivateChild*, translating its state to **inactive**. An element in this state is no longer visible on the screen, and if its state does not change, then **unmount** will be called on it at the end of the animation frame. Such an element becomes **defunct** and can no longer be returned to the tree

Creating elements is an expensive operation and therefore should be reused whenever possible. This is achieved using **Keys**. We'll deal with the keys further, but for now let's get back to InheritedElement and how it notifies other elements that we need to redraw.

Everything is simple, it describes a method that runs through all the dependent elements and calls the notifyDependent function, which in turn calls didChangeDependecies() on the widget

```
void notifyClients(InheritedWidget oldWidget) {
  assert(_debugCheckOwnerBuildTargetEx
ists('notifyClients'));
  for (Element dependent in _dependents.keys) {
  assert(() {
      // check that it really is our descendant
      Element ancestor  dependent._parent;
      while (ancestor ! this && ancestor ! null)
        ancestor  ancestor._parent;
      return ancestor  this;
    }());
    // check that it really depends on us
    assert(dependent._dependencies.contains(this));
    notifyDependent(oldWidget, dependent);
  }
}
```

```
protected
void notifyDependent(covariant InheritedWidget oldWidget,
Element dependent) {
  dependent.didChangeDependencies();
}
```

KEYS

Keys are identifiers of widgets (Widget), elements (Elements), and also semantic nodes (SemanticNode).

When flutter redraws the UI, it goes through the entire hierarchy of elements, comparing the TYPE of the widget and the KEY, so if the type is the same and the key is not set, then there will be nothing to redraw. If the key of a widget associated with the item matches the key of the updated widget, the item will be redrawn.

Keys are divided into local and global: *LocalKey*, *GlobalKey*. Local keys must be unique among elements within their parent. Global keys must be unique throughout the application.

(!)In general, **keys are not needed by StatelessWidgets**. But Stateful-Widgets need them when there are several. For example, in the list.

In order to show how the keys work in Flutter, you have to slightly refactor our project. We will add a screen with a list of places for which you can see the weather.

```
class PlacesPage extends StatefulWidget {
  PlacesPage({Key key}) : super(key: key);

  _PlacesPageState createState()  _PlacesPageState();
}

class _PlacesPageState extends StatePlacesPage {

  // initial test list
  ListPlacemark _places  [
    Placemark(
        name: 'Moscow',
        country: 'Europe',
    administrativeArea: 'Moscow',
        position: Position(longitude: 37.6206, latitude:
55.7532)),
Placemark(
        name: 'Paris',
        country: 'Europe',
```

```
            administrativeArea: 'Paris',
            position: Position(longitude: 2.2950, latitude:
48.8753)),
        Placemark(
            name: 'London',
            country: 'Europe',
            administrativeArea: 'London',
            position: Position(longitude: 0.1254, latitude:
51.5011)),
    ];
```

Next, in the rendering method, pay attention to the line

```
      key: Key(place.name),
```

to the Dismissable widget. **Dismissable** – is a list widget item that can be deleted by swipe right or left. At the same time, in order for the ListView to know how to correctly redraw it, it needs to know which element has been deleted. We set the location name as the key, so Flutter can identify them when redrawing.

```
override
Widget build(BuildContext context) {
  return Scaffold(
    appBar: AppBar(
      title: Text("Places"),
    ),
    body: Column(children: Widget[
      Row(mainAxisAlignment: MainAxisAlignment.start, chil
dren: Widget[
        Expanded(
          child: InkWell(
            onTap: ()  _onItemTapped(null),
            child: Padding(
              padding: const EdgeInsets.all(16.0),
              child: Text("Current position",
                  textAlign: TextAlign.left,
                  style: new TextStyle(
                    fontSize: 16.0,
                    color: Colors.black,
                  )),
            ),
          ),
```

```
          ),
        )
      ]),
      Divider(
        height: 4,
        thickness: 2,
      ),
      Expanded(
          child: ListView.builder(
        itemCount: _places.length,
        itemBuilder: (context, index) {
          final place  _places[index];
          return Dismissible(
            key: Key(place.name),
            onDismissed: (direction) {
              setState(() {
                _places.removeAt(index);
              });
              Scaffold.of(context)
                  .showSnackBar(SnackBar(content: Text("
place removed")));
            },
            background: Container(
              color: Colors.red,
            ),
            child: ListTile(
              title: Text(_preparePlaceTitle(place)),
              onTap: ()  _onItemTapped(place),
            ),
          );
        },
      )),
    ]),
    ***
    );
    ***
}
```

What else interesting here? An **InkWell** widget is just a rectangular area that responds to clicks. That's all, in fact, regarding the **Keys** for today. The topic is quite large, so further work with the list of places that we created will be continued in the next chapter, where we will work with connecting Google Maps packages, as well as TimeZone to add a new location.

LESSON 7. SCREEN NAVIGATION, WORK WITH GOOGLE MAPS

In this chapter:

- Navigation using MaterialPageRoute
- Google Maps integration
- Timezone package integration

NAVIGATION USING MATERIALPAGEROUTE

At this moment we created a screen with a list of places, but did not go to the weather screen. And indeed, many important details related to showing the list of places, their addition and removal were omitted. We are now closing those gaps.

So let's get started. Add the following functions to the *_PlacesPageState* class

```
/// generates a place name based on an [Placemark] object
String _preparePlaceTitle(Placemark placemark) {
  var placeTitle  "";
  if (placemark.country ! null) {
    placeTitle  placemark.country;
  }
  if (placemark.administrativeArea ! null) {
```

```
    placeTitle  placeTitle ", "  placemark.administra
tiveArea;
  } else if (placemark.name ! null) {
    placeTitle  placeTitle  ", "  placemark.name;
  }
  return placeTitle;
}

/// Handler for clicking on a list item  navigate to
weather screen
void _onItemTapped(Placemark place) {
  Navigator.push(
    context,
    MaterialPageRoute(builder: (context)  WeatherForecast
Page(place)),
  );
}

/// Floating button click handler  add a new place
void _onAddNew() async {
  final result  await Navigator.push(
    context,
    MaterialPageRoute(builder: (context)  MapPage()),
  ); // wait for a new added place

  setState(() {
    if (result ! null) {
      _places.add(result);
    }
  });
}
```

A widget called **Navigator** is responsible for navigation in Flutter applications. To perform the screen change operation, you need to call the push method with the MaterialPageRoute parameter in the constructor of which in the lambda of the build method you need to pass the widget (screen) that we want to place on top.

Note that the onAddNew function has the async modifier as well as setState. Thus, we will wait for the result of this screen - the location object, which we will select on the map.

Now add a screen with a map.

GOOGLE MAPS INTEGRATION

Note. It is assumed that you already have com.google.android.
geo.API_KEY. It is needed to receive data from Google servers. If you
do not already have one, then first get it according to the instructions

Add next lines to AndroidManifest.xml

```
metadata android:name"com.google.android.geo.API_KEY"
    android:value"!- YOUR API KEY "/
```

And for iOS in the ios/Runner/AppDelegate

```
GMSServices.provideAPIKey("YOUR API KEY")
```

Next, in the *pubspec.yaml* add

```
google_maps_flutter: 0.5.217
```

And run command

```
flutter packages get
```

Now you may write the code. Create MapPage.dart and add into it:

```
import 'dart:collection';
import 'package:flutter/material.dart';
import 'package:flutter_hello_world/LocationInfo.dart';
import 'package:geolocator/geolocator.dart';
import      'package:google_maps_flutter/google_maps_flut
ter.dart';

class MapPage extends StatefulWidget {
  override
  _MapPageState createState()  _MapPageState();
}

class _MapPageState extends StateMapPage {
  GoogleMapController _mapController;
  Marker positionMarker;
  SetMarker _markers  HashSetMarker();
  Placemark _placemark;
```

```
bool _isLoading  false;
LatLng _markerPosition  LatLng(55.7532, 37.6206);

void _onMapCreated(GoogleMapController controller) {
  _mapController  controller;
}

override
 void didChangeDependencies() {
   super.didChangeDependencies();
   _loadData();
}
```

Map rendering is made by **GoogleMap** widget

```
/// Map rendering is made by widget [GoogleMap]
Widget get _contentView {
  return GoogleMap(
    onMapCreated: _onMapCreated,
    markers: _markers,
    mapType: MapType.normal,
    initialCameraPosition: CameraPosition(
      target: _markerPosition,
      zoom: 11.0,
    ),
    onTap: (latLng)  _updatePlaceMark(latLng),
  );
}
```

At startup, the screen will access the location specified in Inherited-Widget and use it to draw a widget.

```
void _loadData() {
  _isLoading  true;
  _initPlaceMark();
  if (_placemark ! null) {
    setState(() {
      _markerPosition
          LatLng(_placemark.position.latitude, _placemark.
position.longitude);
      reInitMarker();
```

```
      _isLoading  false;
   });
  }
}

/// read data from the InheritedWidget [LocationInfo]
void _initPlaceMark() {
  if (_placemark  null || _placemark?.position  null) {
    // get the data from InheritedWidget
    var locationInfo  LocationInfo.of(context);
    // read placemark variable
    _placemark  locationInfo?.placemark;
  }
}
```

We also add a function that will redraw the marker on the map in case
of a click on the map or moving the marker.

```
/// call this function when tap on the map or moving the
marker
/// update coordinates and location data for marker
void _updatePlaceMark(LatLng latLng) {
  if (_isReinitingMarker) {
  return;
  }
  _isReinitingMarker  true;
  setState(() {
    _markerPosition  latLng;
  });
  var placeFuture  LocationHelper.getPlacemark(
      _markerPosition.latitude, _markerPosition.longi
tude);
  placeFuture.then((newPlaceMark) {
    setState(() {
      _placemark  newPlaceMark;
      _reInitMarker();
    });
  });
}
```

Whole the MapPage screen code you may find in the github repository.

TIMEZONE PACKAGE INTEGRATION

From the weather service, date data comes in the UTC format. In order for the time data for different points of the globe to be displayed correctly, we need to know the timezone (time zone) for a specific location. In the pub.dev/packages there is a timezone (https://pub.dev/packages/timezone). It contains the entire database IANA (https://www.iana.org/time-zones) of time zones and their corresponding coordinates. Let's connect this library.

On the readme page there is a brief instruction for connecting. However, it is incomplete and does not contain all the information. More detailed instructions may be found at Medium (https://medium.com/flutter-community/working-with-timezones-in-flutter-1c304089dcf9)

First add in the **pubspec.yaml**

```
dependencies:
  timezone: 0.5.4
```

Then run the command in terminal

```
flutter pub get
```

After that, you need to go to the folder with the installed packages. In Android Studio, on the right side of the IDE, in the project tree, expand **External Libraries->Dart packages**, then right-click on the timezone package to open the folder in terminal. After that, you need to go to the folder with the installed packages.

In the terminal window, type **cd..** to go up one level and run the command

```
flutter pub run tool/get s 2019b
```

After that, in **pubspec.yaml**, specify the database as a resource.

```
    assets:
            packages/timezone/data/2019b.tzf
```

And the last step: initializing the library. Change the main function so that it looks like this:

```
void main() async {
  WidgetsFlutterBinding.ensureInitialized();
  var byteData  await rootBundle
      .load('packages/timezone/data/2019b.tzf');
  initializeDatabase(byteData.buffer.asUint8List());
  runApp(MyApp());
}
```

Now you can use the library. In our case, we will use it for displaying list items with a forecast - each time must be shown taking into account the time zone. In the getWeather function of the **_WeatherForecastPageState** class we will parse the placemark place in the timezone and take into account the time zone in the element.

```
try {
  var locationZone
    "{_placemark.country}/{_placemark.administrativeAr
ea.replaceAll(" ", "_")}";
  final placeTime
      TZDateTime.from(itCurrentDay, getLocation(location
Zone));
  placeTimeZoneOffset  placeTime.timeZoneOffset;
} on Exception catch (e) {
  placeTimeZoneOffset  deviceTimeZoneOffset;
}
. . .
```

and then set the offset of the timezone to an element, which, as you remember, takes this offset into account when displaying the time:

```
while (iterator.moveNext()) {
  var weatherItem  iterator.current as ListBean;
  weatherItem.timeZoneOffset  placeTimeZoneOffset;
  . . .

DateTime getDateTime() {
  var dateTime  DateTime.parse(dtTxt);
  if (timeZoneOffset ! null) {
      return dateTime.add(timeZoneOffset); /// take into
```

```
account time zone
  } else {
    return dateTime;
  }
}
```

After that, the time for a particular point will be shown considering the time zone.

LESSON 8. SQLITE, CLEAN ARCHITECTURE

In this chapter:

- Connect SQLite
- Implement Repository pattern for places list
- Implement Repository pattern for getting weather forecast

CONNECT SQLITE

We added the ability to add and remove places in the list of places. This is clear, but from the user's point of view it is extremely inconvenient to enter the application and see the list of places unchanged. This happens because it is initialized every time when the application (screen) starts. Now we will do it appropriate, by saving to the local database.

For the Flutter there is an implementation familiar to you – SQLite – represented by package sqflite

Add it into **pubspec.yaml** alongside with path_provider for working with file system

```
sqflite:
path_provider: 1.4.0
```

After executing command *flutter packages get* create file called **db_provider.dart**, and add following class into it

```
class DBProvider {
```

```
DBProvider._();
 static final DBProvider db  DBProvider._();
 Database _database;

}
```

DBProvider – is a singleton, which will provide us with the opportunity to work with the database. We will execute commands by invoking them on an instance of this class.

get database method performs lazy initialization of a class object Database from package:sqflite/sqflite.dart

```
FutureDatabase get database async {
    if (_database ! null) return _database;
    // if _database is null we instantiate it
    _database  await initDB();
    return _database;
  }

 initDB() async {
    Directory documentsDirectory  await getApplicationDocu
mentsDirectory();
    String path  join(documentsDirectory.path, DB_NAME);
     return await openDatabase(path, version: 1, onOpen:
(db) {},
        onCreate: (Database db, int version) async {
      await db.execute(CREATE_PLACES_TABLE);
    });
  }
```

Now add the string constants used for SQL

```
static const String DB_NAME  "flutter_weather.db";

static const String PLACES_TABLE_NAME  "Places";

static const String CREATE_PLACES_TABLE  "CREATE TABLE
PLACES_TABLE_NAME ("
    "id INTEGER PRIMARY KEY,"
    "name TEXT,"
```

```
"isoCountryCode TEXT,"
"country TEXT,"
"postalCode TEXT,"
"administrativeArea TEXT,"
"subAdministrativeArea TEXT,"
"locality TEXT,"
"longitude REAL,"
"latitude REAL,"
"timestamp INTEGER"
")";
```

In order for us to identify place objects, Placemark, we need to give each of them an id. But, since the Placemark class is described in the geolocator package, we will write our wrapper for local storage of places:

```
class PlacemarkLocal {
  int id;
  Placemark placemark;

  PlacemarkLocal({
    this.id,
    this.placemark,
  });

  factory PlacemarkLocal.fromMap(MapString, dynamic map
Str)
      new PlacemarkLocal(
          id: mapStr["id"],
          placemark: Placemark(
            name: mapStr["name"],
            isoCountryCode: mapStr["isoCountryCode"],
            country: mapStr["country"],
            administrativeArea: mapStr["administra
tiveArea"],
            subAdministrativeArea: mapStr["subAdministra
tiveArea"],
            position: Position(
              longitude: mapStr["longitude"],
              latitude: mapStr["latitude"],
              timestamp: mapStr["timestamp"],
```

```
        ),
      ));

  MapString, dynamic toMap()  {
        "id": id,
        "name": placemark.name,
        "isoCountryCode": placemark.isoCountryCode,
        "country": placemark.country,
        "administrativeArea": placemark.administra
tiveArea,
        "subAdministrativeArea": placemark.subAdministra
tiveArea,
        "longitude": placemark.position?.longitude,
        "latitude": placemark.position?.latitude,
        "timestamp": placemark.position?.timestamp?.milli
secondsSinceEpoch,
      };
}
```

And add methods to manipulate data

```
/// place refresh
updatePlacemark(PlacemarkLocal newPlacemark) async {
  final db  await database;
  var res  await db.update(PLACES_TABLE_NAME, newPlace
mark.toMap(),
      where: "id  ?", whereArgs: [newPlacemark.id]);
  return res;
}


/// place adding
getPlacemark(int id) async {
  final db  await database;
  var res  await db.query("Client", where: "id  ?", wher
eArgs: [id]);
  return res.isNotEmpty ? PlacemarkLocal.fromMap(res.
first) : null;
}

/// getting a list of all places
FutureListPlacemarkLocal getAllPlacemarks() async {
  final db  await database;
```

```
   var res   await db.query(PLACES_TABLE_NAME);
   ListPlacemarkLocal list   res.isNotEmpty
       ? res.map((c)   PlacemarkLocal.fromMap(c)).toList()
       : [];
   return list;
}
```

```
/// delete a place
deletePlacemark(int id) async {
  final db = await database;
  return db.delete(PLACES_TABLE_NAME, where: "id = ?", whereArgs: [id]);
}
```

Now, of course, we can add **DBProvider** calls to the **places_page.dart** file. However, this will not be quite correct. It may turn out that our list of places will come from the server. Then you have to rewrite the widget code. Which is completely inconvenient, and with the complex hierarchical structure of widgets in flutter, this task can become difficult and lead to new errors. Fortunately, there is a reliable and proven solution - clean architecture.

IMPLEMENT REPOSITORY PATTERN FOR PLACES LIST

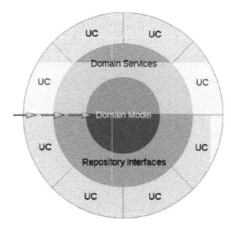

source - commons.wikimedia.org

If you suddenly do not know what clean architecture is, be sure to study this topic separately. In short, we have several levels: the level of the data domain (business logic), the level of interface adapters (controllers, presenters, repositories) and the level of data presentation (UI). The upper layers depend on the lower, but in no case vice versa.

We are now accessing data at the repository level. And UIs (widgets) will access the repository through, for example, a presenter, or, as we will see later, using special **BloC**s.

So, let's create a repository for the list of places. Create a package in the lib repository. And inside it - file **places_repository.dart**

```
class PlacesRepository {
  PlacesRepository();
}
```

Transfer the place list initialization method into it

```
ListPlacemark _initPlaces   [
  Placemark(
      name: 'Moscow',
      country: 'Europe',
```

```
      administrativeArea: 'Moscow',
      position: Position(longitude: 37.6206, latitude:
55.7532)),
  Placemark(
      name: 'New York',
      country: 'America',
      administrativeArea: 'New York',
      position: Position(longitude: 73.9739, latitude:
40.7715)),
  Placemark(
      name: 'Los Angeles',
      country: 'America',
      administrativeArea: 'Los_Angeles',
      position: Position(longitude: 122.4663, latitude:
37.7705)),
  Placemark(
      name: 'Paris',
      country: 'Europe',
      administrativeArea: 'Paris',
      position: Position(longitude: 2.2950, latitude:
48.8753)),
  Placemark(
      name: 'London',
      country: 'Europe',
      administrativeArea: 'London',
      position: Position(longitude: 0.1254, latitude:
51.5011)),
];
```

And we will add methods for working with place objects using the SQLite database through the previously prepared DBProvider

```
FutureListPlacemarkLocal getPlaces() async {
  var placesFuture  DBProvider.db.getAllPlacemarks();
  var placesList  await placesFuture;
  if (placesList.isEmpty) {
    await putPlaces(_initPlaces);
  }
  return await DBProvider.db.getAllPlacemarks();
}

addPlace(Placemark placemark) async {
  await DBProvider.db.addPlace(placemark);
```

```
}

updatePlacemark(PlacemarkLocal newPlacemark) async {
  await DBProvider.db.updatePlacemark(newPlacemark);
}

putPlaces(ListPlacemark places) async {
  for (var place in places) {
    await DBProvider.db.addPlace(place);
  }
}

deletePlacemark(int id) async {
  DBProvider.db.deletePlacemark(id);
}
```

And now we can add to the DBProvider class the methods we need to perform operations on places.

```
/// getting a list of all places
FutureListPlacemarkLocal getPlaces() async {
  var placesFuture  DBProvider.db.getAllPlacemarks();
  var placesList  await placesFuture;
  if (placesList.isEmpty) {
    putPlaces(_initPlaces);
  }
  return await DBProvider.db.getAllPlacemarks();
}

/// adding place
addPlace(Placemark placemark) async {
  await DBProvider.db.addPlace(placemark);
}

/// place update
updatePlacemark(PlacemarkLocal newPlacemark) async {
  await DBProvider.db.updatePlacemark(newPlacemark);
}

/// add a list of places
putPlaces(ListPlacemark places) async {
  for (var place in places) {
    await DBProvider.db.addPlace(place);
  }
```

```
}

/// place removal
deletePlacemark(int id) async {
  DBProvider.db.deletePlacemark(id);
}
```

That's all, the place list repository is ready. We created a class that internally prepares data for the external layer (UI) and emits it. To better understand, we'll create another similar repository for receiving weather data.

IMPLEMENT REPOSITORY PATTERN FOR GETTING WEATHER FORECAST

Add file **weather_repository.dart** with weather repository class:

```
class WeatherRepository {
  final WeatherApiClient weatherApiClient;

  WeatherRepository({required this.weatherApiClient})
      : assert(weatherApiClient ! null);

  FutureForecastResponse getWeather(Placemark placeMark)
async {
    return await weatherApiClient.fetchWeather(placeMark);
  }

}
```

As you can see, the repository simply encapsulates weather data asynchronously. In our case, we directly pull the server using the object of the **WeatherApiClient** class. If we wanted to cache data, then this logic would be here in the repository.

WeatherApiClient is responsible for accessing the server, and we need to transfer to it the code with the request and **httpClient** variable

```
class WeatherApiClient {
  final http.Client httpClient;

  WeatherApiClient({required this.httpClient}) : asser
t(httpClient ! null);

  FutureForecastResponse fetchWeather(Placemark
placeMark) async {
    if (placeMark  null) {
      return null;
    }

  double lat  placeMark?.position?.latitude;
  double lng  placeMark?.position?.longitude;

  var queryParameters  {
      /// prepare request parameters
```

```
    'APPID': Constants.WEATHER_APP_ID,
    'units': 'metric',
    'lat': lat.toString(),
    'lon': lng.toString(),
  };

 var uri  Uri.https(Constants.WEATHER_BASE_URL,
     Constants.WEATHER_FORECAST_URL, queryParam
eters);

 /// perform query and wait for result
  var response  await http.get(uri);

 /// parse JSON and return forecast response
  var forecastResponse  ForecastResponse.
fromMap(json.decode(response.body));

 return forecastResponse;
 }}
```

The repository is ready now, and we can receive data. However, we still need to parse them and, if necessary, map, that is, perform some operations on them, before showing them to the user. We will do this in the same layer using special components - **BloC**s, which will be described in the next chapter

LESSON 9. BLOC, STREAMS

In this chapter:

- BLoC
- Streams
- Use BLoC for the counter example
- Weather application refactoring using BLoC library

BLOC

In all previous examples we changed the state of widgets using the *setState* function. In fact, this is convenient enough when the state of the widget has one or two variables and does not contain complex logic. However, as you probably know, applications in the real world can have quite complex and even confusing business logic, and if you implement all of it in the State class of the widget, you would get a giant, hard-to-support spaghetti code. To implement proper composition and architecture of the code for such a project, we can apply BLoC. What is BLoC?

Literally, it is an acronym for Business Logic Component. It is a component that encapsulates an application's *business logic layer*. This is the same level at which the presenter works in MVP, or rather VeiwModel in MVVM. By the way, VeiwModel is extremely appropriate analogy as alike MVVM, BLoC allows the UI to subscribe to state changes. In short, it can be represented by a simple diagram:

Events arrive at input, and at the output we have State, which is used by Widgets.

What is BLoC in code? In fact, it is just a class with reactive flows within itself, which, in turn, manipulate the data received from outside and allow the UI to subscribe to the result of the calculations.

Here we need to stop and understand in more detail how reactive programming is presented in Dart and what **Stream** is.

STREAMS

Streams are data streams emitted sequentially in an amount from 0 to n. By analogy with RxJava, this is an Observable. This is pure reactivity, which we have in Dart out of the box.

In order to receive data from the Stream, you need to subscribe to it.

```
final _stream  SomeGenerator().stream;
final subscription  _stream.listen(
      (data)  print('data'),
);
```

Important notice: by default, only one listener can subscribe to Stream. So that one Stream can listen to several subscribers, you need to call the **asBroadcastStream** method on the stream.

You can also listen for errors, and there is also a very convenient **cancelOnError** flag that allows the application not to fall in case of an error in the stream. Which is very convenient, and you do not need to write *onErrorReturn* as in RxJava.

```
final subscription = _stream.listen(
    (data) => print('$data'),
    ),
      onError:(err){
            print('err')
      },
      cancelOnError: false,
      onDone:(){
```

```
        print('Done)
    }
);
```

just like in Rx, Streams have a **map** operator, which allows you to filter emitted elements:

```
final subscription = _ SomeGenerator().stream
    .where((data) => data.isValid() == true)
    .map((data) => 'Valid $data')
    .listen(
        (data) => print('$data'),
    );
```

STREAMCONTROLLER

To create a **Stream** manually, you need to use the **StreamController** class. This is a wrapper over the Stream, which allows you to send data to the stream. If we look at the source of the class, then everything is quite simple in it. Stream with generic type and onListen, onPause, on-Resume, onCancel callbacks.

```
abstract class StreamController<T> implements StreamSink<T> {
 /** The stream that this controller is controlling. */
 Stream<T> get stream;


 . . .


 /**
 * The callback which is called when the stream is listened to.
 *
 * May be set to `null`, in which case no callback will happen.
 */
 ControllerCallback get onListen;

 void set onListen(void onListenHandler());

 /**
 * The callback which is called when the stream is paused.
```

```
*
* May be set to `null`, in which case no callback will happen.
*
* Pause related callbacks are not supported on broadcast stream con-
trollers.
*/
ControllerCallback get onPause;

void set onPause(void onPauseHandler());

/**
* The callback which is called when the stream is resumed.
*
* May be set to `null`, in which case no callback will happen.
*
* Pause related callbacks are not supported on broadcast
stream controllers.
*/
ControllerCallback get onResume;

void set onResume(void onResumeHandler());
```

In order to send an event / data to the Stream, you need to call the **sink.add (<data>)** method on the StreamController. We will see later in the example with the counter how this works in practice. For now we will note an important point how to use Stream in the UI.

In order for the widget to be updated in accordance with the changes coming from the Stream, this widget needs to be wrapped in a special **StreamBuilder** widget. StreamBuilder has a *stream* parameter, in which we provide a stream with data, as well as a builder function in which, using the data received from the stream, you can draw a widget.

```
StreamBuilder(
   stream: _myStream,
   initialData: variable,
   builder: (BuildContext context, AsyncSnapshotData type
snapshot) {
```

```
    return Text('{snapshot.variabl}');
  },
),
```

USE BLOC FOR THE COUNTER EXAMPLE

And now, in order to better understand, we'll create BLoC from scratch for our simple counter application from lesson 3.

To start, let's create simple classes that will be increment and decrement events.

```
abstract class CounterEvent {}

class IncrementEvent extends CounterEvent {}

class DecrementEvent extends CounterEvent {}
```

Then create the BLoC class itself. We put in it the value of the counter, which we will change, as well as StreamControllers and streams.

```
import 'dart:async';

import 'package:flutter_hello_world/counter_event.dart';

class CounterBloc {
  int _counter  0;

    final _counterStateController  StreamControllerint();

StreamSinkint get _inCounter  _counterStateController.
sink;

Streamint get counter  _counterStateController.stream;

final _counterEventController  StreamControllerCounter
Event();

SinkCounterEvent get counterEventSink  _counterEventCon
troller.sink;
```

You should already know almost everything besides Sink.

Sink is a generic interface that allows you to put in a data stream. At the end of the stream, you need to call close () on it. That's all it can do. In our case, we will transfer events through it to BLoC. And we will receive the stream from the **Stream counter** stream. Add a constructor and dispose method to our BLoC class.

```
CounterBloc() {
  _counterEventController.stream.listen(_eventToState);
}

void _eventToState(CounterEvent event) {
  if (event is IncrementEvent) {
    _counter;
  } else if (event is DecrementEvent) {
    _counter;
  } else {
    throw Exception('wrong Event type');
  }
  _inCounter.add(_counter);
}

void dispose() {
  _counterStateController.close();
  _counterEventController.close();
}
```

In the eventToState function, we transform the resulting event into business logic data - increment or decrement.

Now that our BLoC is ready, add it to the state of the counter widget.

```
class _CounterWidgetState extends StateCounterWidget {
  final _bloc  CounterBloc();
```

A widget with the text of the current counter value needs to be wrapped in StreamBuilder

```
StreamBuilder(
  stream: _bloc.counter, // Stream from BLoC at the input
  initialData: 0,
  builder: (BuildContext context, AsyncSnapshotint snap
shot) {
    return Text('{snapshot.data}', // get the data via
AsyncSnapshot
        style: TextStyle(fontSize: 20.0));
  },
),
```

Provide the stream from our BLoC as a parameter to **StreamBuilder**.

We get the data through the AsyncSnapshot object, which literally represents an immutable representation of asynchronous computing.

We will also send increment and decrement events to BLoC through button clicks, using counterEventSink

```
IconButton(
onPressed: () {
  _bloc.counterEventSink.add(DecrementEvent());
},
icon: Icon(Icons.remove)),
IconButton(
onPressed: () {
  _bloc.counterEventSink.add(IncrementEvent());
},
icon: Icon(Icons.add)),
```

And finally, add the dispose BLoC in the dispose method of the widget to avoid memory leaks.

```
override
void dispose() {
  super.dispose();
  _bloc.dispose();
}
```

That's all, we implemented the BLoC pattern with a simple example. As you can see, the code of the CounterWidgetState class has become much more concise. This will be especially noticeable with the example of more complex business logic.

WEATHER APPLICATION REFACTORING USING BLOC LIBRARY

The counter example is a bit far-fetched, because the business logic there is the simplest, and the need for BLoC is not so acute there. But if we return to the weather example, then the bloc pattern will come in very handy.

There will be two blocs in our application; one for the list of places and the second for the weather itself.

Note: when designing the application architecture on Flutter, we must strive to ensure that each element of the business logic has its own separate BLoC.

You can add one more for geolocation, however, in our case it is more convenient and easier to use InheritedWidget for the location, so we will leave the location determination code unchanged. So let's go.

In IDE return to branch *lesson_8_bloc* from 8 and add bloc library same as described above for counter example. Then create BLoC classes for weather and places.

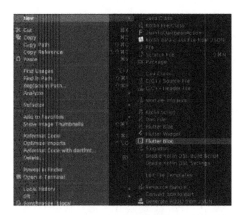

Adding a new BLoC via IDE plugin

First, create the blocs folder. In it, right-click and select *New- Flutter Bloc*. This element was added to us by the plugin. It will generate the base classes of the block. Enter the name of the **Weather** bloc and **OK**.

First, let's define event classes. We will inherit the **Equatable** class from the package **equatable: ^0.6.1**. It implements == and hashCode based on props.

part of 'weather_bloc.dart';

```
immutable
```

```
abstract class WeatherEvent extends Equatable {
  const WeatherEvent();
}

/// weather request
class FetchWeather extends WeatherEvent {
  final Placemark placemark;

  const FetchWeather({required this.placemark}) : assert(
placemark ! null);

  override
  ListObject get props  [placemark];
}

/// refresh weather
class RefreshWeather extends WeatherEvent {
  final Placemark placemark;

  const RefreshWeather({required this.placemark}) : assert(
placemark ! null);

  override
  ListObject get props  [placemark];
}
```

Next, prepare state classes

```
part of 'weather_bloc.dart';
immutable
abstract class WeatherState extends Equatable {
  const WeatherState();

  override
  ListObject get props  [];
}

/// empty list
class WeatherEmpty extends WeatherState {}

/// loading state
class WeatherLoading extends WeatherState {}

/// the forecast is loaded from server
```

```
class WeatherLoaded extends WeatherState {
  final ForecastResponse forecastResponse;

  const WeatherLoaded({required this.forecastResponse}) :
assert(forecastResponse ! null);

  override
  ListObject get props  [forecastResponse];
}

/// error state
class WeatherError extends WeatherState {
}
```

Now that we have both events and states ready, it remains only to map one into the other in the BLoC class. Also, through the constructor, we will transfer to the BLoC class the instance of the repository prepared in chapter 8, with which we will get the weather.

```
class WeatherBloc extends BlocWeatherEvent, WeatherState {
  final WeatherRepository weatherRepository;

  WeatherBloc({required this.weatherRepository})
      : assert(weatherRepository ! null);

  override
  WeatherState get initialState  WeatherEmpty();

  override
  StreamWeatherState mapEventToState(WeatherEvent event)
async* {
    if (event is FetchWeather) {
      yield WeatherLoading();
      try {
        final ForecastResponse response
            await weatherRepository.getWeather(event.place
mark);
        yield WeatherLoaded(forecastResponse: response);
      } catch (_) {
        yield WeatherError();
      }
    }
    if (event is RefreshWeather) {
      try {
```

```
      final ForecastResponse response
      await weatherRepository.getWeather(event.place
mark);
      yield WeatherLoaded(forecastResponse: response);
    } catch (_) {
      yield WeatherError();
    }
  }
}
}
```

The block is ready. It remains to initialize it at application startup, as well as to implement reading and writing data to it on the weather screen.

Add the line to the main class

```
    BlocSupervisor.delegate  BlocDelegate();
```

We initialized the BLoC delegate. It will manage all the BLoCs in the application. Then prepare the place repository.

```
final WeatherRepository weatherRepository  WeatherReposi
tory(
  weatherApiClient: WeatherApiClient(
    httpClient: http.Client(),
  ),
);
```

After that wrap the application in **BlocProvider**

```
runApp(BlocProvider(
  builder: (context)
      WeatherBloc(weatherRepository: weatherRepository),
  child: MyApp(),
));
```

We are done with **main.dart**. Let's move to **weather_forecast_page.dart** and write the state rendering function in it:

```
Widget get _contentView {
  return BlocBuilderWeatherBloc, WeatherState(builder:
(context, state) {
    if (state is WeatherEmpty) {
      return errorView(context, 'No data received. Pull to
refresh');
```

```
    }
    if (state is WeatherLoading) {
      return loadingView();
    }
    if (state is WeatherError) {
      return errorView(context, "Exception while fetching
weather");
    }
    if (state is WeatherLoaded) {
      final weatherResponse  state.forecastResponse;
      if (weatherResponse.cod  200.toString()) {
        initWeatherWithData(weatherResponse.list);
        return _weatherListView;
      } else {
        // в случае ошибки показываем ошибку
        Scaffold.of(context).showSnackBar(SnackBar(
          content:
              Text("Error {weatherResponse.cod} {weatherRe
sponse.message}"),
        ));
        return errorView(
            context, "Error occured while loading data from
server");
      }
    }
    return null;
  });
}
```

In case of successful loading of weather data, we build a ListView wrapped in RefreshIndicator. In the onRefresh function, we will notify the BLoC of the update event.

```
Widget get _weatherListView {
  return RefreshIndicator(
    onRefresh: () {
        BlocProvider.ofWeatherBloc(context).add(
          RefreshWeather(placemark: _placemark), /// add
weather update event to the BLoC
        );
        return _refreshCompleter.future;
```

```
      },
      child: ListView.builder(
          itemCount: _weatherForecast  null ? 0 : _weather
Forecast.length,
          itemBuilder: (BuildContext context, int index) {
            final item  _weatherForecast[index];
            if (item is WeatherListBean) {
              return WeatherListItem(item);
            } else if (item is DayHeading) {
              return HeadingListItem(item);
            } else
              throw Exception("wrong type");
          }));
}
```

We also add the **refreshWrapper** function as a wrapper over the
BlocListener, which will allow us to update the weather using **Completer**

```
Widget get _refreshWrapper {
  return BlocListenerWeatherBloc, WeatherState(
      listener: (context, state) {
        if (state is WeatherLoaded) {
          _refreshCompleter?.complete();
          _refreshCompleter  Completer();
        }
      },
      child: _contentView);
}
```

We have prepared the UI, it remains to load the data. To do this,
change the **getWeather** function as follows:

```
void _getWeather() {
  _initPlaceMark();
  if (_placemark ! null) {
    BlocProvider.ofWeatherBloc(context)
        .add(FetchWeather(placemark: _placemark)); /// add
weather loading event to the BLoC
```

```
    }
}
```

Downloading the weather on this is ready, it remains to add a BLoC for the list of places. Similarly, we create classes for events and for states.

```
part of 'places_bloc.dart';

immutable
abstract class PlacesEvent extends Equatable {
  const PlacesEvent();
}

class FetchPlaces extends PlacesEvent {
  const FetchPlaces();

  override
  ListObject get props  [];
}

class AddPlaceEvent extends PlacesEvent {
  final Placemark placemark;

 . const AddPlaceEvent({required this.placemark}) : assert(
placemark ! null);

  override
  ListObject get props  [placemark];
}

class RemovePlaceEvent extends PlacesEvent {
  final PlacemarkLocal placemarkLocal;

  const RemovePlaceEvent({required this.placemarkLocal})
      : assert(placemarkLocal ! null);

  override
  ListObject get props  [placemarkLocal];
}

part of 'places_bloc.dart';
```

```
immutable
abstract class PlacesState extends Equatable {
  const PlacesState();

  override
  ListObject get props  [];
}

class EmptyPlacesState extends PlacesState {}

class LoadingPlacesState extends PlacesState {}

class LoadedPlacesState extends PlacesState {
  final ListPlacemarkLocal placemarks;

  const LoadedPlacesState({required this.placemarks})
      : assert(placemarks ! null);

  override
  ListObject get props  [placemarks];
}

class ErrorPlacesState extends PlacesState {}

class ErrorAddingPlaceState extends PlacesState {}

class RemovedPlaceState extends PlacesState {
  final int id;

  const RemovedPlaceState({required this.id}) : assert(id
0);

  override
  ListObject get props  [id];
}

class ErrorRemovingPlaceState extends PlacesState {}
```

In PlacesBloc we pass the place repository prepared in chapter 8.

```
part 'places_event.dart';

part 'places_state.dart';

class PlacesBloc extends BlocPlacesEvent, PlacesState {

  final PlacesRepository placesRepository;

  PlacesBloc({required this.placesRepository})
      : assert(placesRepository ! null);

  override
   PlacesState get initialState  EmptyPlacesState();

  override
   StreamPlacesState mapEventToState(PlacesEvent event)
async* {
    if (event is FetchPlaces) {
      yield LoadingPlacesState();
      try {
        final ListPlacemarkLocal places
        await placesRepository.getPlaces();
        yield LoadedPlacesState(placemarks: places);
      } catch (_) {
        yield ErrorPlacesState();
      }
    }
    if (event is AddPlaceEvent) {
      yield LoadingPlacesState();
      try {
        /// add new place
      await placesRepository.addPlace(event.placemark);
        /// get all new places as list to reinit UI
        final ListPlacemarkLocal places
        await placesRepository.getPlaces();
        yield LoadedPlacesState(placemarks: places);
      } catch (_) {
        yield ErrorAddingPlaceState();
      }
    }
    if (event is RemovePlaceEvent) {
```

```
    try {
      /// remove new place
      await placesRepository.deletePlacemark(event.place
markLocal.id);
      yield RemovedPlaceState(id: event.placemark
Local.id);
    }catch (_) {
      yield ErrorRemovingPlaceState();
    }
  }
 }
}
```

Now we need to change the initialization of BlocProvider in main.dart.
First, add the line

```
final PlacesRepository placesRepository  PlacesReposi
tory();
```

Then we will replace BlocProvider with **MultiBlocProvider**, because
now we have 2 blocks, not one.

```
runApp(MultiBlocProvider(
  providers: [
    BlocProviderWeatherBloc(
      builder: (context)  WeatherBloc(weatherRepository:
weatherRepository),
    ),
    BlocProviderPlacesBloc(
      builder: (context)  PlacesBloc(placesRepository:
placesRepository),
    ),
  ],
  child: MyApp(),
));
```

Next in the **places_page.dart** rewrite the code for receiving and editing
the list of places. In the state initialization method, we add the event of
loading the list of places.

```
override
void initState() {
  super.initState();
  BlocProvider.ofPlacesBloc(context).add(FetchPlaces());
}
```

And the content creation function will look like this:

```
Widget get _contentView {
  return BlocBuilderPlacesBloc, PlacesState(builder: (con
text, state) {
    if (state is EmptyPlacesState) {
      return errorView(
          context, 'No places  yet. Tap Add button to cre
ate one');
    }
    if (state is LoadingPlacesState) {
      return loadingView();
    }
    if (state is ErrorPlacesState) {
      return errorView(context, "Exception while reading
places");
    }
  if (state is ErrorAddingPlaceState) {
      showSnackBar(context, _scaffoldKey, "Exception while
adding place");
    }
    if (state is LoadedPlacesState) {
      _placemarksList  state.placemarks;
    }
    if (state is RemovedPlaceState) {
      var index  1;
      for (int i  0; i  _placemarksList.length; i) {
        if (_placemarksList[i].id  state.id) {
          index  i;
          break;
        }
      }
      if (index  0) {
        _placemarksList.removeAt(index);
      }
    }
    if (state is ErrorRemovingPlaceState) {
      showSnackBar(context, _scaffoldKey, "Exception while
deleting place");
    }
    return _placesListView;
  });
```

```
}
```

The add and delete functions will also work with the BLoC:

```
/// Floating button handler  add a new place
void _onAddNew() async {
  final result  await Navigator.push(
   context,
    MaterialPageRoute(builder: (context)  MapPage()),
  ); // wait for added place
  BlocProvider.ofPlacesBloc(context).add(AddPlaceEvent(
placemark: result));
}

/// handler for removing an item from a list
void _onRemoveItem(int index) {
  BlocProvider.ofPlacesBloc(context)
      .add(RemovePlaceEvent(placemarkLocal: _placemark
sList[index]));
}
```

That's all, run!

From the user's point of view, nothing has changed, but we have significantly refactored the code, and this made our life easier - our code has become more supportable and has gained proper architecture.

LESSON 10. DI, TESTS

In this chapter:

- Dependency Injection in the Flutter
- Inject dependencies in the weather example
- Unit test
- UI test
- Integration tests

DEPENDENCY INJECTION IN THE FLUTTER

You already know how to write applications on Flutter. In this final lesson, we will study another important, previously unreported, aspect of software development - testing. As programmers, you should be aware that tests fall into three types: *unit tests*, *UI tests*, and *integration tests*. Later in this chapter, we will analyze them in turn in the context of Flutter. However, first we need to prepare our code. In order to test a separate section of the application, it is necessary that the objects on which this section depends on are instanced outside. So we can substitute the mocked dependencies of the tested object. At the same time, we will bring our code in accordance with the principle of Single Responsibility. According to it, a component — a function, class, or module — must be responsible for one thing, and all the dependencies of this component must be created externally and provided to this component externally.

Enough theory on this, let's try it in practice.

Several DI libraries have already been written for Flutter and Dart, you can find and use any of them at pub.dev. In this course we will connect a simple and lightweight package injector (https://pub.dev/packages/injector):

```
dependencies:
    injector: 1.0.8
```

Run command **flutter pub get** after **pubspec.yaml** change and open **main.dart**

In the main() add **initInjector();** funciton call before creation of the **SimpleBlocDelegate** and declare the method itself.

```
void initInjector() {
  // get the static instance of the injector
  Injector injector  Injector.appInstance;
  // register instance of a http.Client in the dependency
tree
  injector.registerSingletonhttp.Client((injector) {
    return http.Client();
  });
  // register instance of a WeatherApiClient in the depend
ency tree
  injector.registerSingletonWeatherApiClient((injector) {
    var httpClient  injector.getDependencyhttp.Client();
    return WeatherApiClient(httpClient: httpClient);
  });
  // register instance of a WeatherRepository in the
dependency tree
  injector.registerSingletonWeatherRepository((injector) {
    var webApiClient  injector.getDependencyWeatherApiCli
ent();
    return WeatherRepository(weatherApiClient: webApiCli
ent);
  });
  // register  PlacesRepository object in the dependency
tree
  injector.registerSingletonPlacesRepository((injector) {
    return PlacesRepository();
  });
```

```
}
```

Now let's change the BloC code a bit, injecting dependency using the constructors:

```
class WeatherBloc extends BlocWeatherEvent, WeatherState {
  WeatherRepository weatherRepository;

  WeatherBloc() {
    Injector injector  Injector.appInstance;
    weatherRepository  injector.getDependencyWeatherReposi
tory();
  }
 . . .

class PlacesBloc extends BlocPlacesEvent, PlacesState {
  PlacesRepository placesRepository;

  PlacesBloc() {
    Injector injector  Injector.appInstance;
    placesRepository  injector.getDependencyPlacesReposi
tory();
  }
 . . .
```

Done. Now our code is built on the dependency inversion principle! And we can completely switch to tests.

UNIT TESTS

Unit tests allow you to test a small atomic section of code: function, class, method. In order to implement unit tests in an application, you need to import a package **test**. It contains the basic functionality for testing code in the Dart language, without taking into account the specifics of Flutter. For a practical example, let's go back to the counter example.

By default in the pubspec.yaml there are already present tests import:

```
dev_dependencies:
  flutter_test:
    sdk: flutter
```

Therefore, we leave pubspec unchanged, and in the test folder create the **counter_test.dart** file with the contents:

```
import 'package:flutter_hello_world/counter_bloc.dart';
import 'package:flutter_test/flutter_test.dart';

void main() {
  CounterBloc counterBloc;

  /// called before tests
  setUp(() {
    counterBloc  CounterBloc();
  });

  /// called after test completion
  tearDown(() {
    counterBloc.dispose();
  });
}
```

We imported the test package, and also prepared the **setup** and **teardown** functions, which are invoked before and after the tests, respectively. We also added a counter block object, which we will test.

Add now the test function itself:

```
test('Counter test', () {
  counterBloc.counterEventSink.add(IncrementEvent());
  expect(counterBloc.counter, emits(1));
});
```

Here we dispatch the increment event, and wait for bloc to return a one. That's all. Right-click on the file with the test and in the drop-down menu we find *Run Tests* in **counter_test.dart** Click and look at the results.

Tests passed. Be sure to get the same result message.

MOCKITO

Let's go back to the branch with the weather application and create a test for the weather repository class - WeatherRepository. In order to simulate (mock) the server, we need the **mockito** package:

```
dev_dependencies:
  flutter_test:
    sdk: flutter
  mockito: 4.1.1
```

When an object inherits from the Mock class, all declared and non-implemented methods will receive implementation. That is, if the function *Future<Response> getWeather()* is declared in the class, then in the mocked form the object will return Future with the answer.

We will mock http client. To do this, you need to inherit or mix the Mock class, as well as implement the target class:

```
import 'package:flutter_test/flutter_test.dart';
import 'package:mockito/mockito.dart';
import 'package:http/http.dart' as http;

class MockHttpClient extends Mock implements http.Client
{}

main() {
  setUp(() {});

  tearDown(() {});
}
```

Add the objects of the repository and the WeatherApiClient necessary for it:

```
class MockAPIClient extends Mock implements WeatherApiClient {}

main() {
```

```
   WeatherRepository weatherRepository;

  setUp(() {
     final httpClient  MockHttpClient();
     final apiClient  MockAPIClient();
     weatherRepository  WeatherRepository(weatherApiClient:
apiClient);
   });
```

To simulate a response, simply copy an example server response
from the openWeather website: https://openweathermap.org/fore-
cast5 into a constant:

```
const   String   successJson      '{"city":{"id":1851632,"
name":"Shuzenji","coord":{"lon":138.933334,"
lat":34.966671},"country":"JP","timezone":        32400,
"cod":"200","message":0.0045,"cnt":38,"list":
[{"dt":1406106000,"main":{"temp":298.77,"tem
p_min":298.77,"temp_max":298.774,"pressure":1005.93,"sea_
level":1018.18,"grnd_level":1005.93,"humidity":87,"temp_k
f":0.26},"weather":[{"id":804,"main":"Clouds","descrip
tion":"overcast         clouds","icon":"04d"}],"clouds":
{"all":88},"wind":{"speed":5.71,"deg":229.501},"sys":
{"pod":"d"},"dt_txt":"20140723 09:00:00"}]}';
```

Also add a place test object, and initialize the Uri variable:

```
var testPlacemark  Placemark(
    name: 'test',
    country: 'test',
    position: Position(longitude: 0, latitude: 0));

var uri;
```

The setup method will look like this:

```
setUp(() {
  mockClient  MockHttpClient();
  apiClient  WeatherApiClient(httpClient: mockClient);
  weatherRepository  WeatherRepository(weatherApiClient:
apiClient);

  double lat  testPlacemark?.position?.latitude;
  double lng  testPlacemark?.position?.longitude;
```

```
var queryParameters  {
   // prepare request parameters
  'APPID': Constants.WEATHER_APP_ID,
   'units': 'metric',
   'lat': lat.toString(),
   'lon': lng.toString(),
 };

 uri  Uri.https(Constants.WEATHER_BASE_URL_DOMAIN,
     Constants.WEATHER_FORECAST_PATH, queryParameters);
});
```

Now we need to simulate a successful and unsuccessful server response. In order to run several tests at once, you can use the **group** function

First, add a test of successful request to it.

```
test('success response test', () async {
  // Return successful result
  when(mockClient.get(uri)).thenAnswer(
     (_) async  http.Response(successJson, 200, headers: {
        HttpHeaders.contentTypeHeader: 'application/
json; charsetutf8'
        }));

  var response  await weatherRepository.getWeather(test
Placemark);
  // check that the answer came in the form of [Respon
seWrapper]
  expect(response, isInstanceOfResponseWrapper());
  // and contains correct [ForecastResponse]
  expect(response.forecastResponse, isInstanceOfForecastRe
sponse());
  expect(response.errorResponse, null);
  expect(response.forecastResponse.city.name, "Shuzenji");
});
```

As we already know, **when** keyword sets the rules. In our case, the rule is: "When trying to query for the matching uri, issue prepared json **successJson**." Further, in the expect blocks, we check our response and its contents for compliance with the required class type and the correctness of the data.

Add similar test for the case of an error request:

```
test('returns error message', () async {
  // Return unsuccessful result
  when(mockClient.get(uri)).thenAnswer(
      (_) async  http.Response('{"message":"Not Found"}',
404, headers: {
          HttpHeaders.contentTypeHeader: 'application/
json; charsetutf8'
          }));

  var response  await weatherRepository.getWeather(test
Placemark);
  // check that the answer came in the form of [Respon
seWrapper]
  expect(response, isInstanceOfResponseWrapper());
  // and contains [ErrorResponse]
  expect(response.errorResponse, isInstanceOfErrorRe
sponse());
  expect(response.forecastResponse, null);
  expect(response.errorResponse.message, "Not Found");
});
```

Now, in the Run Configurations menu, select Flutter Test and run

You should see a message **Tests passed**

UI TESTS

Flutter UI tests are called Widget tests, and their essence is to make sure that a separate widget looks and behaves as expected from it. Widgets have their own lifecycle, respond to user actions, draw themselves, and may also contain other widgets. Therefore, UI tests are more complex than Unit test.

In the **pubspec.yaml** we already have required package import flutter_test

It contains the components we need:

WidgetTester – a class, which allows you to create widgets and interact with them in a test environment.

testWidgets – function in which we will write the tests. This function will be used instead of the *test* function that we wrote for unit tests.

Finder and **Matcher** constants - allows you to find a widget of a particular class and separate it among other widgets of the same class.

Let's go back to the example with the counter in the *lesson_3_counter* branch and create the **counter_widget_test.dart** file in the test folder:

```
import 'package:flutter_test/flutter_test.dart';

void main() {
  // testWidgets function will run tests and provides a
WidgetTester
  // object, which allows to create widgets
  testWidgets('Counter widget test', (WidgetTester tester)
async {
    // tests goes here
  });
}
```

Create a widget for our application with a counter. To do this, use the **pumpWidget** function of the **WidgetTester** class.

```
await tester.pumpWidget(MyApp());
```

To control the life cycle of a widget, for example, when we need to redraw the widget, or to call build on it again in a test environment, use the **pump()** and **pumpAndSettle()** methods

The difference between them is that **pump()** calls the build widget once, while **pumpAndSettle()** calls rendering until the animation frames end in the queue.

In order to gain access to its properties and to itself after creating the widget, you need to use the **find** functions. So, we will find a widget with text - the value of the counter, and make sure that it is 0 at the start.

```
expect(find.text("0"), findsOneWidget); // finds widget
expect(find.text("1"), findsNothing); // fails to find
```

Next, make sure that we have a counter widget and tap on it:

```
expect(find.byIcon(Icons.add), findsOneWidget);

await tester.tap(find.byIcon(Icons.add));
```

Now, since the state of the widget has changed, you need to call **pump()** so that the **build** method is called on the widget

```
await tester.pump();
```

And it remains to be sure that the value has increased:

```
expect(find.text("1"), findsOneWidget);
```

Run the test!

Whole test code:

```
import 'package:flutter/material.dart';
import 'package:flutter_hello_world/main.dart';
import 'package:flutter_test/flutter_test.dart';
```

```
void main() {

  // testWidgets function will run tests and provides a
WidgetTester
  // object, which allows to create widgets
  testWidgets('CounterWidget test', (WidgetTester tester)
async {

    await tester.pumpWidget(MyApp());

    // Make sure that the value of counter at the start is
0, not 1
    expect(find.text("0"), findsOneWidget);
    expect(find.text("1"), findsNothing);

    // Make sure the plus button is present
    expect(find.byIcon(Icons.add), findsOneWidget);

    // click on the add button
    await tester.tap(find.byIcon(Icons.add));
    // waiting for the widget to be drawn after clicking
the button
    await tester.pump();

    // Make sure that the counter value has increased to one
    expect(find.text("1"), findsOneWidget);

  });
}
```

INTEGRATION TESTS

Integration tests – these are literally combined, complex tests that are performed on the entire application or subsystem at once. Such a test usually involves launching the application on a real device or emulator, performing business logic actions, such as querying the server and / or writing to the database. Integration tests can be especially useful for automatic testing in CI (Continuous Integration) - they can be run on the build server for each assembly automatically or according to a schedule, checking the specified sections of the application, without requiring the participation of human testers.

So let's get started. Integration tests run as a separate process, so the sequence of steps for writing tests will also be slightly different. Add lines to pubspec.yaml

```
dev_dependencies:
    flutter_driver:
      sdk: flutter
    test: any
```

Next, create a **test-driver** folder, and a **app.dart** and **app-test.dart** inside it

First file – **app.dart** – will represent an instrumental (run using a device or emulator) app version. Second file – **app-test.dart** – will contain, the test intself. In the app.dart write following:

```
import 'package:flutter_driver/driver_extension.dart';
import 'package:flutter_hello_world/main.dart' as app;

void main() {
  // Connect driver_extension
  enableFlutterDriverExtension();

  // Call `main()` function
  app.main();
}
```

Before writing a test, add the key to the **places_page.dart** file for the first element of the list that shows the weather for the current location:

```
child: Text("Current position",
    key: Key('current_position'),
```

Now in the **app_test.dart** add code

```dart
import 'package:flutter_driver/flutter_driver.dart';
import 'package:test/test.dart';

void main() {
  group('Weather app test', () {
    // Via Finder find widget Text with 'current_position' key
    final currentPositionTextFinder  find.byValueKey('current_position');

    FlutterDriver driver;

    // Connect to the Flutter driver
    setUpAll(() async {
      driver  await FlutterDriver.connect();
    });

    // After performing the test, turn off
    tearDownAll(() async {
      if (driver ! null) {
        driver.close();
      }
    });

    test('Current position, () async {

      // wait 3 seconds for the list of places to load
      sleep(Duration(seconds: 3));

      // Make sure the widget contains the appropriate text
      expect(await driver.getText(currentPositionTextFinder), "Current position");
    });

  });
}
```

And run from the terminal using the command

```
flutter drive targettest_driver/app.dart
```

Note: You must have a device connected or an emulator running.

The test driver will install and start the application on the emulator itself: and make sure that the tests work out. We look at the emulator and make sure that the test does its job, and in the logs we see the success of the test:

```
Using device Android SDK built for x86.
Starting application: test_driver/app.dart
Initializing gradle...                                    4.0s
Resolving dependencies...                                14.6s
Installing build/app/outputs/apk/app.apk...               3.3s
Note: Some input files use unchecked or unsafe operations.
Note: Recompile with -Xlint:unchecked for details.
Running Gradle task 'assembleDebug'...
Running Gradle task 'assembleDebug'... Done             23.6s
Built build/app/outputs/apk/debug/app-debug.apk.
Installing build/app/outputs/apk/app.apk...               3.5s
I/flutter (17222): Observatory listening on http://127.0.0.1:340...
00:00 +0: Weather app test (setUpAll)
[info ] FlutterDriver: Connecting to Flutter application at http://127.0.0.1:...
[trace] FlutterDriver: Isolate found with number: 683728079177147
[trace] FlutterDriver: Isolate is paused at start.
[trace] FlutterDriver: Attempting to resume isolate
[trace] FlutterDriver: Waiting for service extension
[info ] FlutterDriver: Connected to Flutter application.
00:01 +0: Weather app test starts at 0
I/flutter (17222): Transition { currentState: EmptyPlacesState, event: FetchPlaces, nextState: LoadingPlacesState }
I/flutter (17222): Transition { currentState: LoadingPlacesState, event: FetchPlaces, nextState: LoadedPlacesState }
00:03 +1: Weather app test (tearDownAll)
00:03 +1: All tests passed!
Stopping application instance.
```

The test was successful. But it was a simple test. We will write a more complex and close to the real world. It will check that by pressing the button Current Position the weather screen will open and it will be loaded from the server. To do this, add the second test to the group. In it, we will click on the current position button, then we will wait for the weather to load, making sure that we have the list loaded in the List-View, and the list itself will scroll down to the n-element.

```
test('Loading weather for current location', () async {
  // Click on the current weather widget
  await driver.tap(currentPositionTextFinder);

  // wait for 5 seconds until the weather and the screen load
  sleep(Duration(seconds: 5));

  // Find the weather list
  final listView = find.byValueKey('weather_listview');
  // Since our forecast consists of 5 days with 7 elements in each,
  // then the list will have at least 30 lines, and the 30th line will be at the end
```

```
  final thirtyElement  find.by
ValueKey('weatherListItem_30');

  // make sure the list scrolls until the third day with
the weather
  await driver.scrollUntilVisible(
    // Specify the list as a parameter
    listView,
    // And the item we are looking for
    thirtyElement,
    // Using a negative dyScroll value scroll the list down
    dyScroll: 200.0,
  );

  sleep(Duration(seconds: 2)); // just waiting to realize
our success });
```

Start with the same command and look in the terminal.

Success!

CONCLUSION

You have mastered the basic skills required to develop mobile applications on Flutter. Congratulations!

Flutter – is a relatively young technology, but every year it is becoming stronger, and the ranks of Flutter developers are replenished with more and more programmers. We don't know what the world of mobile development will be like in 10 years, and whether Flutter will become the main tool for creating cross-platform applications, but today it is possible to write truly cross-platform code for iOS and Android in production using it. At the same time, nothing stands still, and nowadays almost no one writes code for mobile applications in Java and Objective-C. Many are switching or have already completely switched to Kotlin and Swift, which are more lightweight, easier and convenient. Similarly, no one will now write a frontend on Fortran or pure C. The world is changing, languages and platforms are changing. It is possible that in 10 years everyone will write in Dart, or another unified language, for new devices with universal interfaces. In any case, the world of exciting innovations and solutions awaits us, and I wish you not to miss the appearance of promising technologies and tools, but to have time to study them and put them into practice for cool, successful projects. Good luck!

If you have any questions or suggestions, feel free to ask them on the forum of the FlyFlutter.ru project in the section devoted to this book.

USEFUL LINKS

All the code for this book is in the github repository:

https://github.com/acinonyxjubatus/flyflutter_fast_start

Lession 1. Launch Flutter

Code for the chapter in the branch *lesson_1_hello_world*

Lession 2. Dart programming language

For a more detailed acquaintance with the language, all its rules with keywords, operands, it is recommended to visit the official website of the language: https://dart.dev/

Detailed article about compiling on Flutter: https://proandroidde-v.com/flutters-compilation-patterns-24e139d14177

Lession 3. StatelessWidget and StatefulWidget

Code for the chapter in branches *lesson_3_1_stateless, lesson-_3_1_stateful*

https://flutter.dev/docs/development/ui/layout

StatelessWidget creation tutorial https://medium.com/flutter/how-to-create-stateless-widgets-6f33931d859

Lession 4. ListView creation

Code for the chapter in the branch: *lesson_4_listivew*

Using Packages and Libraries in Flutter Applications: https://flut-ter.dev/docs/development/packages-and-plugins/using-packages

ListView articles: https://medium.com/@DakshHub/flutter-displaying-dynamic-contents-using-listview-builder-f2cedb1a19fb

https://fidev.io/flutter-listview/

https://flutter.dev/docs/cookbook/lists/mixed-list

https://api.flutter.dev/flutter/widgets/ListView-class.html

Lession 5. Loading data from server

Code for the chapter in the branch: *lesson_5_http*

Data mapping: https://flutter.dev/docs/cookbook/networking/background-parsing

Asynch / Await: https://www.youtube.com/watch?v=SmTCmDMi4BY

Streams: https://www.youtube.com/watch?v=nQBpOIHE4eE

Network data loading: https://flutter.dev/docs/cookbook/networking/fetch-data

Asynch / Await: https://dart.dev/codelabs/async-await

Lession 6. Inherited Widgets, Elements, Keys

Code for the chapter in the branch: *lesson_6_inherited*

Inherited Widgets: https://ericwindmill.com/using-flutter-inherited-widgets-effectively

https://flutterbyexample.com/set-up-inherited-widget-app-state/

https://medium.com/@mehmetf_71205/inheriting-widgets-b7ac56dbbeb1

https://medium.com/flutter/keys-what-are-they-good-for-13cb51742e7d

https://www.youtube.com/watch?v=Eca-RIpQrvE

Keys: https://medium.com/flutter-community/elements-keys-and-flutters-performance-3ef15c90f607

Lession 7. Screen navigation, work with Google Maps

Code for the chapter in the branch: *lesson_7_navigation_maps*

Google Maps integration in Flutter: https://codelabs.developers.google.com/codelabs/google-maps-in-flutter/#5

https://medium.com/flutter/google-maps-and-flutter-cfb330f9a245

Timezone package import: https://medium.com/flutter-community/working-with-timezones-in-flutter-1c304089dcf9

Lession 8. SQLite, Clean Architecture

Code for the chapter in the branch: *lesson_8_sqlite_clean_architecture*

SQLite in Flutter: https://flutter.dev/docs/cookbook/persistence/sqlite

Clean architecture: https://blog.cleancoder.com/uncle-bob/2012/08/13/the-clean-architecture.html

Lession 9. BLoC, Streams

Code for the chapter in the branch: *lesson_9_bloc, lesson_9_1_counter_bloc*

Bloc library: https://bloclibrary.dev/#/gettingstarted

Bloc library article: http://flutterdevs.com/blog/bloc-pattern-in-flutter-part-1/

Lession 10. DI, Tests

Code for the chapter in the branch: – *lesson_10_di_tests, lesson-_9_1_counter_bloc*

Dependency injection: https://en.wikipedia.org/wiki/Dependency_injection

https://blog.usejournal.com/compile-time-dependency-injection-in-flutter-95bb190b4a71

Testing: https://flutter.dev/docs/testing

Integration testing: https://flutter.dev/docs/cookbook/testing/integration/introduction

Unit-тесты bloc: https://medium.com/flutter-community/unit-testing-with-bloc-b94de9655d86

Unit-test, integration tests, review article: https://blog.usejournal.com/integration-and-unit-testing-in-flutter-f08e4bd961d5

--

The book uses fragments of the source code of the FlutterTM framework. The license is available at https://github.com/flutter/flutter/blob/master/LICENSE

Flutter and the related logo are trademarks of Google LLC.

We are not endorsed by or affiliated with Google LLC.